Praise for A Simple Choice

"If you think you have learned all you need to know about living simply, think again. *A Simple Choice* offers new insights, refreshing common sense and the author's firsthand experience...don't hesitate on this one—many delightful discoveries await you!" **Linda Breen Pierce, author of** *Choosing Simplicity: Real People Finding Peace and Fulfillment in a Complex World*

"People who long for a life beyond chasing time and money will appreciate the hope *A Simple Choice* offers. More than a how-to guide for living on a limited income, this book is a common sense toolbox for strengthening personal and family priorities." **Karen Jogerst, author of** *If I Could Just Get Organized! Home Management Hope for Piles and Filers!*

"Finally a truly practical application to the simple abundance philosophy. *A Simple Choice* is the perfect marriage of simple living, philosophy and hands-on day-to-day living within ones' means. This book will help you regain control over your life!" **Angie Zalewski, cofounder, Frugal Family Network**

"*A Simple Choice* shows us that living a life of simplicity is not a life of impoverishment, but can be a life of great richness. Taylor-Hough offers us many suggestions that will allow us the time to bring more joy into our lives." **Keith C. Heidorn, Ph.D., ACM, Publisher of** *Living Gently Quarterly*

"This book describes how to successfully pursue both the simple and frugal lifestyles. Deborah's tried-and-true tips reveal how simplicity and frugality can live happily ever after." **Jonni McCoy, author of** *Miserly Moms*

"Even when we know we need to slow down and find a way to simplify our lives, we often lack the knowledge of how to accomplish this elusive but needed change. Friendly, helpful and real, *A Simple Choice* covers every aspect of simplification. This book truly will save your 'time, money and sanity.'" **Catherine Levison author of *A Charlotte Mason Education* and *More Charlotte Mason Education***

"*A Simple Choice* is a power-packed resource guide for saving your time, money and sanity. I've never before found such an exhaustive source or practical money and time-saving tips, housekeeping strategies, inexpensive family activities, household management skills and practical solutions for everyday living! This book is a must-have for every family." **Penny E. Stone, author of *365 Quick, Easy and Inexpensive Dinner Menus***

"You'll not only learn why you'd like to live simply, but what you stand to gain and how to do it. A wonderful primer for those who want to take control of their lives." **Gary Foreman, *The Dollar Stretcher***

"For those wanting to simplify their lives, *A Simple Choice* lives up to its subtitle: 'a practical guide for saving your time, money and sanity!' Families will find practical solutions for the challenges of day-to-day living." **Maggie Dail, Educational Consultant**

"Taylor-Hough does a fine job of meshing the practical with the philosophical. Those seeking a simpler lifestyle need to hear more than just the 'whys', but also the 'hows' of simplification. Deborah does this in a way that is palatable and easy to digest for bot h beginners and veteran simplifiers alike." **Nancy Twigg, Editor, *Counting the Cost Newsletter***

A Simple Choice

a practical guide for saving
your time, money and sanity

Other books by Deborah Taylor-Hough

Frozen Assets: how to cook for a day and eat for a month

A Simple Choice

a practical guide for saving your time, money and sanity

Deborah Taylor-Hough

CHAMPION PRESS, LTD.
WASHINGTON ~ CALIFORNIA

Dedication

This book is dedicated to my mother, Joan Burak Taylor, who's courage, humor and profound faith in the midst of overwhelming difficulties will always be the greatest inspiration to me. She fought the good fight. She finished the course. She kept the faith.

CHAMPION PRESS, LTD.
CALIFORNIA ~ WASHINGTON

Library of Congress Catalog Card Number 00-131034

ISBN 1-891400-49-5

Cataloging-in-Publication Data
Taylor-Hough, Deborah.
     A simple choice : a practical guide for saving
your time, money, and sanity / Deborah
Taylor-Hough -- 1st ed.
     p. cm.
     Includes bibliographical references.
     LCCN: 00-131034
     ISBN: 1-891400-49-5

     1. Home economics. 2. Cookery
3. Housekeeping. 4. Time management. 5. Simplicity.
I. Title.

TX147.T39 2000   640.41

Manufactured in Canada.
10 9 8 7 6 5 4 3 2 1
Book and Cover Design by Calbro.

Acknowledgments

I mainly want to thank the hundreds of people who responded to my on-line and email surveys. I wish it were possible to thank each of you by name for all the time and effort you put into completing those questionnaires. And I'd also like to express my appreciation to the participants on the Simple Living Quips and Frugal Tips message board. Your thoughts and tips continue to be helpful, inspirational and encouraging. I believe there's wisdom in a multitude of counselors. Thank you for offering to share your wisdom and advice.

I would also like to thank:

Larry Wilson
You're the best List Administrator I could asked for. Thank you for everything!

Karen Jogerst
My hat's off to you, Filer/Piler Lady! You accomplished what no one else could do—you got my laundry room organized!

Lisa Morales
Some friends make the world more special just by being in it. Thank you so much for your contributions to this book and for the inspiration of your life.

Catherine Levison
So many conversations. Friend to friend, writer to writer, C.W to R.W. It's all been so helpful. But above all else, I'm glad we found a way to cut those phone bills in half! Spud.

Gina Dalquest

Thank you for being there to laugh, cry, chat, tell stories and brainstorm at all hours of the day (and night!). What would I do without you . . . and without your "famous" Pizza Blanks recipe?

Brook Noel

It's been quite a year, hasn't it? Thank you for your patience, encouragement and help—you're the best! By the way, who's that woman in the dark glasses lurking around the grocery store aisles?

My Family

You're the reason this is possible. I love you all so much! Thank you for everything.

Contents

Part One: Getting Started

CHAPTER ONE / Personal Thoughts on Simplicity 3

CHAPTER TWO / Defining Simplicity 6

CHAPTER THREE / Are You Spiritually Overextended? 10

CHAPTER FOUR / Are You Financially Overextended? 14

CHAPTER FIVE / What's Your Mission? 19

    Seasons of Life 20

    An Official Statement of Purpose 23

    Writing Your Family Mission Statement 24

Part Two: The Path to Financial Health

CHAPTER SIX / Solving Payment Problems 31

    Ten Simple Steps to Conquer Debt 32

    Letter to Creditors 34

CHAPTER SEVEN / Spending Plans 36

    General Budget Guidelines 37

    Money is a Tool 38

CHAPTER EIGHT / Contentment 40

CHAPTER NINE / One Income Living

    in a Two Income World 44

    The Secret 45

    What it Takes 47

Part Three: The Simplified Kitchen

CHAPTER TEN / An Introduction to Frozen Assets 51

    Small Freezer Syndrome 53

    Top Ten Questions 54

    Cooking with a Friend 57

    Freezer Meal Potluck 58

    Lunches 59

Recipes 61

CHAPTER ELEVEN / Saving on Meal Expenses 63

    Breakfast 63

    Lunch 64

    Dinner 65

    Making the Most of Leftovers 66

CHAPTER TWELVE / Grocery Savings 68

    Super Coupon Shopping 73

CHAPTER THIRTEEN / Homemade Alternatives 76

    Mix-n-Match Skillet Meal 76

    International Sausage Skillet 78

    Instant Coffee Recipes 78

    Cream Soup Substitute 79

    Dry Onion Soup Mix 79

    Frozen Pop Recipes 79

    Ice Cream Sandwiches 80

    Swedish Oven Pancakes 81

    Buttermilk Pancakes 81

    French Toast Casserole 82

    Bean Soup Mix 82

Part Four: Simplified Housekeeping

CHAPTER FOURTEEN / Simplified Housekeeping 87

    Ten Minute Tidy 88

    "Times Up" Upkeep 89

    Pink Bunnies 90

    Toys 92

    The Kitchen 92

    Quick Housekeeping Tips 93

    Bedroom and Closet Tips 96

    Garage Tips 97

    Kitchen Tips 97

Laundry Tips	98
CHAPTER FIFTEEN / Pilers and Filers	99
The Piles of My Life	100
Identifying the Piles	101
Containing the Piles	102
CHAPTER SIXTEEN / Kids and Clean Up	104
Job Descriptions	105
Chore Charts	107
Check Mark System	107
CHAPTER SEVENTEEN / Garage Sales	110
Number of Days	111
Classified Ads	111
Stuff	112
Arrangement of Sale	113
Clothing	114
Soft Background Music	114
Odds-and-Ends Tips	115
CHAPTER EIGHTEEN / Homemade Alternatives	117
Fabric Softner	117
Glass Cleaner	117
Drain Cleaner	117
Laundry Liquid Recipe	117
Automatic Dishwasher Soap	118
Windshield Washer Solution	118
Spa Milk Bath	119
Facial Mask	119
Fizzing Bath Bombs	119

Part Five: Simple Family Fun

CHAPTER NINETEEN / Simplify the Holidays	123
CHAPTER TWENTY / Family Fun and Games	130
Keep a Straight Face	130

Spot the Thimble   130

Musical Spoons   131

Pig Pile Chairs   131

Noah's Ark   131

Strike-a-Pose   132

Mannerisms   132

International Shopper   132

Build a Story   132

Add a Drawing   133

Dozens of Family Fun Ideas   133

CHAPTER TWENTY-ONE / Nature Connections   138

Observations   139

Backyard Bird Survey   140

Nature Notebooks   140

CHAPTER TWENTY-TWO / Homemade Alternatives   144

Homemade Paper   144

Craft Dough   146

Bubbles   146

Crazy Crayons   146

Soap Crayons   147

Homemade Stickers   147

Sidewalk Chalk   147

APPENDIX A / Recommended Resources   149

APPENDIX B / Why Simplicity?   159

BIBLIOGRAPHY   179

Part One
🍃 Getting Started 🍃

CHAPTER ONE

🍃 Personal Thoughts on Simplicity 🍃

"Finding our own inner point of order, our own organizing principle, is a vital step toward simplicity, for whatever we put at the center of our personal solar system is destined in some sense to become the reigning factor in our lives."—Claire Cloninger, *A Place Called Simplicity*

Simplicity can mean so much more than just a simple budget or an unadorned lifestyle. One of the reasons I choose to live a simpler lifestyle is to allow more time in my days for the things I feel are important.

Time for family.

Time for community.

Time for friends.

Time for joy.

And time to be available to others who are in need.

Several years ago when my mother passed away, I became increasingly aware of how busy most people are in this modern world. I know that my friends cared about the grief and pain my family experienced, but I found that only those who had chosen to live a simpler, less complicated lifestyle had the time and opportunity to reach out to us with real acts of love, compassion and helpfulness.

One friend of mine said to me, "I know you need me to be there for you right now, but I'm just too busy. Everything on my plate is urgent and important. I simply have no time! Unfortunately, I won't be there for you through this. But I do care."

And I know that in her heart, she did care. Please don't think I'm complaining. I've just observed that busy people don't usually have time for others when they're in need.

This situation caused me to reevaluate the things that take up my time and energy. Are they essential? Truly essential? If I'm so busy that I can't take a meal to a sick friend, or pay a visit to a grieving family, or even send a card of sympathy or good wishes, then in my eyes, I'm too busy. And there have been times in my life that I've been too busy.

I find that I now try to make choices based on my own personal criteria. When I get to the end of my life, I'd like people to say that I was a great friend and was available when someone had a need.

My busy friend had a home business, many church and community commitments, and a young family to raise. I commend her, but my personal priorities require different choices for my own life. I wouldn't necessarily choose a different path, but just take smaller, thoughtful and more manageable steps along the way.

I also have a home business. I have church and community involvements. I have a family to raise, but I also have time to live my life and really enjoy it. I have time to be there when someone needs more from me than just warm thoughts being sent their way. Good intentions don't count for much—only the things we actually do matter in the end.

I want to have time to do.

I want to have time to love.

I want to have time to live.

As the old saying goes, we make time for those things that are important to us. I want to make time.

In the book, *Gift from the Sea*, Ann Morrow Lindbergh states, "I have learned by some experience, by many examples, and by the writings of countless others before me, that certain environments, certain modes of life, certain rules of conduct are more conducive to inner and outer harmony than others. There are, in fact, certain roads that one may follow. Simplification of life is one of them."

In this book we will focus on some of the simplicity paths you can take to climb out of personal bankruptcy—whatever form that bankruptcy might take in your situation. We will look at effective ways of gaining control of finances through focused priorities and simplified lifestyles, and we will examine how to use focus, planning and priorities to regain control of an emotionally-stressed life.

Both financial and emotional overload are issues of over-commitment and lack of personal focus. Although they might seem like different issues on the surface, many of the solutions for both problems remain the same. Someone who is facing a severe financial problem can actually find their financial situation is creating a feeling of bankruptcy in other areas of life as well.

Oftentimes, all it takes to add joy and sanity back into our lives is just slowing down the pace of our frantic lives for a moment or two. We'll find that when we live by our personal priorities, examine our needs, and discover points of focus, we can help bring order to our lives. The path of simplicity will take us on a journey to a place of joy, fulfillment and peace.

CHAPTER TWO

🍃 Defining Simplicity 🍃

"Activities and disciplines may swirl around us with such velocity that our feet barely touch solid ground." —Jean Fleming, *Finding Focus in a Whirlwind World*

A simple lifestyle can encompass many aspects of life. I've discovered there are as many different styles of simplicity as there are people interested in the topic. After checking the dictionary definitions of simplicity and interviewing over a hundred people while preparing this book, I've come up with a general sense of how people are applying this terminology to their lives.

Simple can mean pure and unadulterated, not mixed with anything else—a straightness of purpose and purity of intention. In *Gift from the Sea*, Lindbergh writes about how she wants to find a central core to her life which will enable her to carry out her assorted obligations and activities well. Simple living could mean a person has chosen to live their life true to a set of priorities they always keep before them, being careful not to mix their priorities with those of the world around them. Simplicity can be a pure life, lived according to personal convictions and free from duplicity or false appearances.

When defining simplicity, a woman in San Diego said, "simplicity is not merely about where I shop, whether I do or do not spend my money, or what I eat. To me, simplicity has a lot to do with finding a center in a world that has become increasingly frenetic all of my life. To live simply is to place my money, time, attention, involvement and energy into that which I love and am passionate about—rather than the myriad of things that flicker past me in a moment."

Simple can mean whole and complet e, free from lack. A simple life takes into account the whole person and their entire life. Keeping balance in all things and maintaining a fullness of life that acknowledges all areas of life—physical, mental, emotional, relational and spiritual. A woman in California writes, "I feel that I've gained a lot by using our money and time wisely. Strength of character and simple wisdom will teach upcoming generations to survive without becoming dependent on the wrong people, things or ideas."

A simple life can mean having enough, but not necessarily having everything. A life that's full and complete doesn't mean that a person has attained everything they've ever dreamed of acquiring or doing in their life. A woman in Singapore wrote, "For me, simple living is more a refocusing of priorities in life. First, I recognized that there were certain things I hoped to achieve (setting up a home, further studies, provision for family, building up a nest egg). Then, I reminded myself that the resources I had were limited. I eventually sat down and decided which goals were short term and which were long term. I started to see that it's only logical to realize I can't have everything I want. I find that life becomes so complicated when you believe that everything is equally important. You allow yourself to be persuaded by family, friends and advertisements that you have to own a certain thing (larger car, latest phone, hottest nail polish color). Ultimately, if you truly examine your life, you'll realize that these extras are just simply that—extra."

Someone who lives simply can also be choosing a life free from useless ornamentation; a life that isn't rich or showy. The Amish come to mind as prime examples of this lifestyle. They live in an unassuming and unpretentious manner. They're humble, not showing off for the benefit of others. A person doesn't have to forfeit all modern conveniences to live a life that isn't glitzy or ostentatious.

Choosing to focus on the inner life of a person rather than the outer trappings of wealth and glamour is also a valid expression of the simple life. A full-time mother in Virginia says, "I actively choose to center our lives around home, church, family and friends and no longer concern myself with everyone else's opinion of my 'wasted career' (advanced graduate degree and abandoned high-power career), or seemingly old-fashioned values. In my opinion, there's nothing more modern than this yearning for simplicity and peace." Another homemaker in Nebraska writes, "Simplicity means not complicated, overblown or flamboyant. Not necessarily current, but not feeling the pressure to be. Simplicity stresses minimum effort in more trivial matters for the purpose of giving more of myself to matters of the heart."

Choosing to eat simple foods and wear simple clothing expresses this choice as well. A woman in southern California said that simplicity has allowed her family to learn to appreciate life's simple pleasures without spending exorbitant amounts of money to keep up with the neighbors. After her husband lost a well-paying job, she says, "There's a great feeling of accomplishment that comes from getting by on less money, from making things yourself, and doing without unnecessary things. Even though we sometimes barely pay the bills, we are much happier than we were when money was plentiful." To a part-time teacher in Washington State simplicity means "enjoying life to its fullest, taking advantage of a spring day to teach my daughter about trees—or being calmed by a light rain. Looking at simple methods of living—creating your own clothes and supplies, growing your own food, and taking advantage of what nature provides for us."

By voluntarily limiting choices, people can often find the ability to focus more fully on the ideas and activities they've chosen to allow into their lives. A pastor's wife in Pennsylvania says, "simplicity means discovering what is important to one's self, and making that the focus of life—not spending time on insignificant pursuits. Simplicity provides a clarity of purpose, less time to take care of material possessions, more time spent with people and activities that matter to me."

Simple can also mean free from difficulty. That doesn't necessarily mean a simple life will be easy, but a simple life can be free from many of the stresses and difficulties inherent in modern life. When something is stated in simple language, it means it's easy to understand and apply.

Simple living can make life easier to understand as our priorities and choices stand out more readily in the midst of calm rather than when they are lost in busyness and chaos. A registered nurse and single mother from Virginia writes, "to me simplicity means easy, without difficulty or hassles. I have an extremely busy life, I work two jobs and have two active children who use me as their personal chauffeur. I've chosen to simplify my life in the area of household chores and meals."

Simple living can mean we've focused on bringing order to how we use our time, how we organize our lives, doing away with clutter and balancing our often conflicting commitments. Many people choose to simplify their lives in order to find time for important things, or to organize their daily lives better so they can spend time pursuing relationships or hobbies. A Human Resources Manager in California writes, "Simplicity means having a lot of free time on the weekends to enjoy life: simple meals (I'm a complete freezer-meal convert!), simple clothes (little dry cleaning and ironing), simple make-up, simple shoes. I was tired of rushing home from work and eating dinner late, doing mounds of dishes every night and then spending weekends shopping and running errands. I want to enjoy life along the way."

Uncluttering our lives in all areas can bring tremendous joy by helping us find an uncluttered spirit as well as an uncluttered home. An Indiana resident (originally from Australia) says, "I have less stuff to worry about being broken or stolen; less to dust and clean; time to think of more important things like family and friends; and time to just be." Angie Zalewski from Texas, co-founder of the Frugal Family Network, writes, "simplicity means the ability to gain freedom over 'stuff' and the control of materialism. Simplifying has helped us de-stress."

Simple living. Finding focus for our lives. This is our focus in the upcoming pages. It is my hope that you'll discover some enriching ideas to help restore a bit of sanity and focus to your busy life. For further inspiring examples of what simplicity looks like in the lives of real people, be sure to check out Appendix B—*The Many Faces of Simplicity*. Before we move into the solutions, let's first evaluate where you are, both financially and spiritually.

CHAPTER THREE

🍃 Are You Spiritually Overextended? 🍃

"If you've identified yourself as too busy, step off that jet-propelled treadmill. Take some time to catch your breath and confront the condition of your soul." —Jean Fleming, *Finding Focus in a Whirlwind World*

Many times we don't experience the joys of life as fully as we can because we're too wrapped up in the busyness and daily-ness of life. With so many conflicting complications tearing at the framework of our lives, is it any wonder we sometimes long to escape to a desert island and experience a little bit of that refreshing, slower-paced "island" time?

Do you find that you feel owned by your over-packed schedule and commitments instead of owning and scheduling your life and activities? Do you feel pulled in a few hundred different directions at once? Do you sense that life is going by and you're not really living it true to yourself or your personal convictions? If so, you may be suffering from spiritual bankruptcy. Life throws so much at us, we often feel like we have no choice but to knuckle down under it all. I've frequently heard people say busyness is just a fact of modern life, and we'd just better learn to handle it or discover how to thrive in the midst of chaos. Family responsibilities, careers, daycare, household chores, meal planning, bills, errands, health issues, car pools, school functions, sports, phone calls, traffic jams, community demands, church committees, political races, taxes, debt. These are just a few of the numerous—and often difficult—demands bombarding us daily.

It can be difficult to find balance in the midst of all these activities, but finding focus is necessary. In order to function properly and reap full satisfaction and enjoyment from our busy lives full of activities, relationships and commitments, we need to understand our internal priorities. While we can't ever free ourselves fully from all of life's demands, we can discover a sense of balance in our lives. Or we can identify ways to shift between the two extremes—finding a time and place in our lives and hearts for contemplation, and then alternating that with other times of busyness and distraction. In *Gift from the Sea*, Lindbergh describes this balancing act as the process of finding a rhythm of life with more creative pauses.

If you're wondering if you personally need to reexamine the amount of distractions, commitments and activities in your life, take the following quiz.

1. Do you sometimes feel a general lack of enthusiasm about life?

2. After a long day at work, are you too exhausted to feel you're dealing effectively with the demands of home and family?

3. Are you worried or anxious about your level of consumer debt?

4. Do you thrive on the adrenaline rush of being busy, but sometimes worry that if one more thing happens, you might not be able to handle it all?

5. Do you use drugs or alcohol to unwind on a regular basis?

6. Is your Daily Planner booked solid everyday?

7. Do you watch more than five hours per week of television?

8. Do you get less than adequate sleep on a regular basis?

9. Do you exercise less than three times per week?

10. Do you dread being kept waiting at an appointment since that extra twenty minutes will throw off your entire day's schedule?

11. Are you behind in any of your bills?

12. Do you have difficulty making time for your spiritual priorities (quiet time, church attendance, study, meditation, prayer)?

13. Do you feel in bondage to your job?

14. Do you feel in bondage to debt?

15. Do you frequently wish there were more hours in the day?

16. Do you dread unexpected events because you have no extra room in your life to handle them?

17. Do you feel that relaxation is a waste of time?

18. Do you have creative talents that aren't being used?

19. Do you desire to be involved helping your community, but don't have time or energy?

20. Do you sometimes feel overwhelmed with clutter?

21. Do you lack inner peace?

22. Do you struggle with feeling discontent?

23. Do you envy those with more material possessions?

24. Do you wish you had more time to reach out to your friends and family when they're in need?

25. Do you need to schedule appointments with your spouse and/or children?

How many times did you answer "yes" to these questions?

0 - 2 YOU'RE ON A LEISURELY DRIVE THROUGH THE COUNTRY-SIDE. Your life isn't out of control and you probably feel good about the choices you are making on how you're spending time, energy and financial resources. I'd love to read your book on simplifying life!

3 - 6 YOU'RE PROCEEDING A BIT TOO FAST. While you probably still feel in control of your life and time, sudden events may surprise you

and cause you to swerve off course, possibly even crashing off the road into a ditch if the events are heavy and strong enough.

7 - 10 NOW YOU'RE TRAVELING BY AIR AND TAKING OFF THE GROUND WITH SEVERE TURBULENCE AHEAD. You're no longer in the driver's seat of your life, someone else (or something else—debt, time constraints, stress) is in the cockpit—and the ride is getting rough. As much as you might like to steer your life through the turbulent air surrounding you, it's difficult to actually grab the steering mechanism because it's really outside of your control. If the plane should start to go down due to unforeseen circumstances, you'll have a difficult—if not impossible time—regaining control in time to prevent disaster.

11 - 25 YOUR JUMBO JET IS ABOUT TO CRASH! Danger! Not only have you lost control of the steering of your life, you're headed for a serious crash on a very fast plane. Being overburdened with time, energy and money constraints is causing your plane to nose dive. It's time to get the plane back to the hangar immediately. It might even require the help of someone else to land the jet safely as you reevaluate your mode of transportation before heading out on your life journey again (find a trained pilot used to dealing with emergency situations—perhaps a financial advisor, a trained personal counselor or a pastor).

CHAPTER FOUR

🍃 Are You Financially Overextended? 🍃

"The problem of money dogs our steps throughout the whole of our lives, exerting a pressure that, in its way, is as powerful and insistent as any other problem of human existence. And it haunts the spiritual search as well." —Jacob Needleman

People facing serious debt problems are under tremendous stress. They feel as if their creditors own them. They feel in bondage to their debts. Their lives are governed by what they owe and the over-commitments they've made to their creditors.

In 1996, for the first time in history, one million personal bankruptcies were filed in the United States. Unfortunately for millions of people, the numbers keep going higher every year. What is at play here? According to financial planner, Ron Blue, debt problems are often the symptom of something else: lack of security, lack of significance, lack of discipline or lack of contentment.

I'm intimately acquainted with the financially bankrupt scenario. Our family faced a serious debt crisis awhile back, mainly due to hospital bills relating to premature babies. Although we had health insurance, it didn't cover more than a small amount of the total medical bills we faced. Intensive Care Nurseries aren't cheap, and much to our surprise, we discovered (after the baby was born), that our insurance had changed and no longer paid for newborn nursery care.

Although our goal was for me to be home full-time with our new baby, we found ourselves struggling to stay afloat financially with our new load of debt. I continued working part-time, but even that didn't seem to be enough to stay ahead of the game. An occasional late payment here and there, and before we knew it, we were facing angry creditors demanding payment yesterday.

Since we weren't sure where else to turn, we called a local nonprofit credit counseling service and sought help. They were able to arrange a more manageable payment schedule, but things were still too tight for us to manage financially from paycheck to paycheck. After much soul searching, we contacted a bankruptcy attorney about looking into filing a Chapter Thirteen Bankruptcy (a wage-earner repayment plan) which would force our creditors to legally accept what we could afford to pay each month. Because of our strong commitment to our Christian faith, we believed filing a Chapter Seven Bankruptcy (the complete liquidation of all of our debts) wasn't an option for our particular family. We rightfully owed the money to our creditors and needed to find some way to repay them. Our attorney advised strongly against trying to repay our debts. He honestly couldn't see how we could manage a five year repayment plan that didn't even allow money in the budget for clothing. He thought we were a bit foolish to even attempt repaying the debts, but we needed to be true to our personal convictions.

Several years before all this happened, we had leased a nice little car. As we looked over our budget ruthlessly in preparation for the Chapter Thirteen filing, we decided the only way we could make it work would require us to turn back in our new car and try to find some sort of transportation we could purchase in cash. With only two hundred dollars to spend on a car, you can guess that we didn't get anything nice. My pride took a severe kick whenever I drove around in that old car. But it was paid for completely, and we could continue to live true to our family priorities, even if it was a bit embarrassing driving around town.

The anticipated repayment schedule for our bankruptcy filing was five years, but due to several unforeseen windfalls and the refunds from our taxes each year, we had the entire sum repaid in four years. At the end of the repayment time, we were sent a certificate from the court that stated that all of our debts were now "paid in full!" I thought seriously about framing that certificate and hanging it on the wall. It had taken a great deal of hard work, unwavering commitment and some personal embarrassment, but we successfully repaid our creditors in spite of the dire warnings from our attorney.

By repaying our debts, we've found a freedom that is almost beyond words. It's such a wonderful experience to no longer have debts hanging over our heads, no nasty creditors calling at all hours of the day and night, and no more sleepless nights wondering how to dig our way out of the horrible mess of a heavy personal debt load.

While I would never recommend contacting a bankruptcy attorney as a first step in personal debt recovery, sometimes it can become a reality that some people may need to face. There are several debt counseling services that can also be of help. We'll examine the options for getting your debt under control in Chapter Six.

It isn't just those who have an existing debt problem that need to be concerned. Those who are continually overspending will also want to take this quiz. One woman I know has plenty of assets yet for what she is making, she should have many more. By examining her spending choices and why she chooses to spend her money on the things she does, she was able to stop spending on items that didn't align with her priorities and save more money for what was important to her like family vacations.

Take the following quiz to find out where you stand financially.

1. Do you regularly pay for groceries with a credit card?

2. Do you spend money now, expecting your income to increase in the future?

3. Do you hide purchases from your spouse or other family members?

4. Do you make only the minimum payment on your credit cards, rather than paying your bill in full each month?

5. Do you have difficulty imagining your life without credit?

6. Are you becoming an expert at juggling each month, deciding which bills to pay and which ones to let go until the next paycheck?

7. Do you feel richer carrying several credit cards?

8. Do you pay off your monthly credit-card bills, but let other bills slide, such as medical expenses and utilities?

9. Have you taken cash advances on one credit card to pay monthly payments on other cards?

10. Do you feel anxiety when you think about or discuss your financial situation?

11. Do you have little or no money in savings?

12. Do you make frequent impulse purchases?

13. Does your installment debt (not including mortgages) amount to more than 20 percent of your income?

14. Has the stress of your financial situation caused severe turmoil in your relationship with your spouse, or other family members?

15. Are you at your credit limits?

16. Do you fail to keep an accurate record of your purchases?

17. Have you applied for more than four credit cards in the past year?

18. Have you started to receive collection letters, notices or phone calls?

19. Do your liabilities exceed your assets?

20. Do you frequently buy things on credit because you cannot afford to pay cash?

21. Are you afraid to answer the phone in case it is a collection agency?

22. Does the idea of living within your means seem impossible?

23. Do you tend to "shop" to feel better?

How many times did you answer "Yes," to the preceding questions?

1 - 5   YOU STILL HAVE A GREEN LIGHT. You can probably proceed in relative safety. Your splurging is not out of control, yet.

6 - 10   SLOW DOWN! You have a flashing yellow light and have entered the caution zone. You need to start exercising self-discipline. It's time to draw up a budget, pay off your debts and reevaluate your spending habits before you find yourself in over your head.

11 - 15   RED LIGHT! STOP! You seriously need to gain control of your spending before you proceed any further. Ignoring the problem will not make it go away. You would be wise to seek out a credit counselor or financial planner for immediate help in changing your spending habits. You are well on the road to financial catastrophe, but there is still hope. Turn around now.

16 - 23   DANGER!! You are careening out of control and emergency measures are needed. You are about to experience a financial crash of monumental proportions. You need to slam on your brakes and come to an immediate stop. The wisest course of action when you find yourself on the wrong road is to turn around and go back. If you keep heading the way you are, you will only go further away from financial stability. If you are this far down the wrong road, you should cut up all of your credit cards and close the accounts, now! Do not spend one more penny on anything but the most basic necessities until you have called a credit counselor for assistance. Do not run out and purchase something today, thinking that you are about to cut up your credit cards! That's the type of thinking that brought you down this road to begin with. Remember, you are not a bad person for being in this situation, but you have made some big mistakes. Now is the time to start making proper decisions about your finances. You can get off this ride, but if you do not take immediate steps to fix the problem, you could soon be another personal bankruptcy statistic.

CHAPTER FIVE

🍃 What's Your Mission? 🍃

"When we neglect the most important priorities, our final reward will be all the unhappiness money can buy." ~Richard A. Swenson, M.D., *Margin*

One of the most important aspects of simplifying your life is identifying your personal set of priorities. Often we can find ourselves so caught up in the busyness and urgent demands of life that we lose track of those things we hold dear and believe to be truly important. Then, when we least expect it, life throws a curve into our plans, helping us focus on life's priorities once again. Many times a crisis will precipitate the refocusing: the loss of a job, the end of a relationship, a change in our health, or even the death of a loved one.

Recently, Margaret (the 16-month-old daughter of some friends of ours) died due to complications from a near drowning incident. Since Margaret's death, I've found myself hugging my children a bit tighter and generally realizing how brief life can be and how important the people around us are.

In the thoughtful book, *A Place Called Simplicity*, Claire Cloninger writes, "when a child is ill or a close friend dies or an all-important relationship is in trouble, there are no gray areas anymore. It suddenly becomes easy to see what is primary and what is merely peripheral. But what a shame that we must wait for a crisis to get our priorities in order. Our lives would be so much easier if we would take the time to look closely at our lives and begin focusing on the important things before a crisis comes."

I'd like to suggest that each of us spend a few uninterrupted quiet moments evaluating the activities that clutter our lives. These various activities may be important and good, but are they truly in keeping with our personal priorities for life? Do they add to, or subtract from, our personal goals? What are your goals? Can you state them clearly and with certainty? What do you want people to say when looking back at your life?

In his book, *Margin: Restoring Emotional, Physical, Financial and Time Reserves to Overloaded Lives*, Richard A. Swenson, M.D. writes, "we would not call it progress if we gained in wealth but lost in relationships; we would not call it beneficial if we improved in estate but lost in relationships; we would not call it profitable if we achieved a promotion but lost spiritual integrity."

The life of little Margaret can actually serve as a model for us. During her brief time here on Earth, this young child loved life and lived it fully. She laughed wholeheartedly. She cried when she was sad. She ate ice cream with wild abandon. She loved her family, and gave hugs and smiles freely. She brought joy to all of us who knew her.

At the end of my life, I don't want people to say, "She was always busy. She had a tremendous career. She was president of this-or-that committee, etc." I'd rather they say something like, "She touched the lives of others and had time for those in need. She brought hope and healing to hurting people. She knew how to laugh—and even how to cry. She ate ice cream with abandon. She loved her family, and gave hugs and smiles freely. And she brought joy to all who knew her."

Seasons of Life

When my first child was born, I was involved in a wide variety of activities. I was working part-time at a local hospital. I volunteered at an agency that offered peer counseling and support groups for women in crisis. I answered a hot-line in my home. I facilitated study groups. I was the Nursery Director and Preschool Sunday School teacher at our church. Additionally, I did all the normal wife/mother/homemaker things, too.

Busy, busy, busy, busy.

You know what happened? I did too much and I burned out—completely and totally. I burned out emotionally, spiritually and physically. I even wound up with a terrible case of pneumonia that put me out of commission for nearly ten weeks. This forced me to stop everything for awhile.

I discovered through all of this that I was in a season of life called "being a Mommy." I became fully aware it was only for a short season of life that my children would be small—and I was convinced that for a season, my focus would need to be on my home life and on my children. All those other activities I had been pursuing with gusto were good and helpful, and even important, but for me, being with my babies was even more important and a higher priority for that season of life.

Our family went through some really hard times. We learned a lot of lessons—the kind only learned through adversity. I also felt that I was supposed to be faithful to the small things put before me like cooking, cleaning, educating my children, praying, reading, studying, being there for my friends and immediate neighbors.

One day, before I'd finally stepped out of my over-commitments, I saw in my mind a picture of my life. I was sitting in the center and all around me whirled assorted activities that made up my busy days. I suddenly noticed that not only my activities, but also my closely held personal priorities, were circling. It dawned on me that maybe these priorities (family, God, service to others) needed to be set firmly in the center hub of the wheel and I needed to make sure that the activities circling my life were actually revolving around my priorities, rather than just around me and my personal schedule.

I discovered that in order to be true to my personal priorities at that time of my life, I needed to focus on being a wife and a mother. I also need to focus on the spiritual aspects of my life. My life had been busy with service to others, but I found even after I shifted my focus to my home life, opportunities for service continued to enter my life.

Service to others became a natural outgrowth of my life, rather than a title on a name tag or a job description at church or one more "to-do" item on a list in my day planner.

I recently read a wonderful little book called *Finding Focus in a Whirlwind World* by Jean Fleming. The author says that she sits down about three or four times each year and reevaluates her various activities in light of her priorities. She said some seasons of life are full of busyness and we just can't help it (sometimes that's just the way life is—hectic and full), but other times we need to be sensitive to possibly needing to sit quietly and focus on quieter pursuits for a time.

In her book, Fleming compared her life to a tree. The trunk of the tree was her number one priority (which in her case was a strong commitment to God). Out of the trunk grew the main limbs which were the main activities of her life (parenthood, career, etc.). Then from the main limbs grew those little branches that had a tendency to grow and multiply quickly. The little branches were the general activities that would crowd in and fill up her day. Just like a tree grows healthier and more fruitful by regular pruning, Fleming saw her times of reevaluating her activities as that time of pruning her life to make it more fruitful. She found it more productive to do a few things well, rather than being involved with a myriad of conflicting activities, but not being fully fruitful with any of them.

I learned a valuable lesson about pruning and fruitfulness in my own front yard. One year, I pruned back a Clematis plant that was overgrowing the front of the house. I cut it back almost to the stump. My husband and neighbors all thought I'd killed the poor plant. To be honest, sometimes I also wondered if maybe I'd been a little overzealous in my pruning.

The following Spring when the Clematis bloomed, it was absolutely breathtaking. Almost every vine had an overabundance of blossoms. It was simply a mass of flowers—unlike anything I'd ever seen. People walking by on the sidewalk would stop to comment on how full and beautiful my plant was that year. But I know that if I hadn't pruned the Clematis back to the bare essentials, it would've continued to grow long and gangly, never achieving the level of beauty and fullness that came from focusing all its energy and growth into it's stem and main branches.

An Official Statement of Purpose

In business enterprises throughout the world, it's a common policy to write a corporate statement of purpose or a Mission Statement. To be able to see and read the expressed purpose and mission of a company allows everyone to be on the same page and to keep the same goals in mind as they work. All corporate decisions can be made in light of the company's carefully defined and written mission statement.

Likewise, each family has a general purpose or mission, whether it's stated on paper or not. The process of actually defining and writing out an official Family Mission Statement can go a long way toward focusing a family's sense of priorities and goals. Having a Mission Statement allows each member of the family to realize their family is an entity in itself, with clearly defined goals. It's not just a group of individuals going their own separate ways, but it's actually a group with an identity and purpose all its own. A Mission Statement can help balance the lives of the people involved, enabling them to clearly see a pattern for living out their commitments, relationships and work-related responsibilities.

Some families have strong religious beliefs that take center stage in their personal view of priorities and outreach to others. Others have a deep desire to touch their community and world in the areas of social welfare or volunteerism. Some families find their focus in maintaining tightly knit and supportive bonds between the individual members of the family, building a strong sense of love and fellowship within the four walls of their homes.

Whatever your family's personal priorities, seeing them written down is an excellent way to keep on track as a group. The actual process of coming up with an official Family Mission Statement can sometimes be the most enlightening and beneficial aspect of this whole idea.

Writing Your Own Family Mission Statement

To start the process of coming up with a Family Mission Statement, you need to sit down and list your top priorities. If you are married or committed to someone, ask them to do this as well. Each write up your own separate list. Be as specific as you can. Take all the time you need to do this well. Be sure to take into account the general shape of your life, the activities and priorities that are part of who you are on a daily basis such as spouse, children, home, career, background, education, moral conscience, faith and creative pursuits.

After you've come up with your Personal Priority List look carefully at your results. If you've done this with a partner, come back together and discuss your results. This part of the process can be eye-opening. It's important to be gracious with each other when any differences appear. Agree ahead of time that no matter how unusual one person's priorities might seem to the other, no one will laugh, ridicule, argue or get angry. One man I spoke with in Portland, Oregon told me that when he and his wife sat down to write a Family Mission Statement, his number one priority was outreach to the community. On his wife's Personal Priority List, that particular priority didn't even show up. At that point they needed to exercise tremendous patience, graciousness and understanding with each other as they worked together to write a mission statement that would encompass both of their personal value systems.

The Family Mission Statement will generally be a compilation of your Personal Priority List, or if you did the exercise with a partner, the Personal Priority Lists you and your partner each came up with. The Family Mission Statement might not contain everything on both of your lists because some of your personal priorities will be just that—personal, only applicable to your individual life. But even then, you'll want to make certain that your Family Mission Statement allows for the expression of the various individual priorities expressed by each of you.

If your children are very young, a Family Mission Statement can be written by the adults in the house working together without the children's direct input. If you have teens or older children still at home, it would be beneficial to include them in the process of drafting the Family Mission Statement. If nothing else, before the Family Mission Statement is finalized, allow the children or teens to read it for themselves and make constructive comments or personal suggestions.

Examples

Family Mission Statements should be relatively short, no longer than one single-spaced typewritten page. The Statement can even be as short as a single sentence or a concise paragraph, quickly and easily summing up the family's mission. Some families have chosen a favorite quotation or even an appropriate scripture verse for their Family Mission Statement.

Your Family Mission Statement should sum up the basic tenets of your family, the beliefs and values that all decisions and rules should be based upon. The Mission Statement itself will not be a list of rules, but it will serve as a list of guiding principles. The assorted specific rules concerning conduct, chores, proper attitudes, etc., may develop out of the Family Mission Statement, but the Mission Statement itself isn't a list of do's and don'ts.

An example of a Mission Statement written for a country rather than a corporation or family, can be found in the Preamble to the Constitution of the United States. It says, "We the people of the United States, in order to form a more perfect Union, establish justice, insure domestic tranquillity, provide for the common defense, promote the general welfare, and secure the blessings of liberty to ourselves and our posterity . . . ." The Preamble (Mission Statement) itself doesn't contain the exact how-to's of those topics mentioned (establishing justice, insuring domestic tranquility, providing for the common defense, etc.). The Preamble sets the tone and states the purpose for the Constitution that follows (the Constitution is then the list of the "rules" for the country that stem from the purpose described in the Preamble).

One family uses a favorite verse of scripture as their Family Mission Statement. It reads, "The most important commandment is this: Love the Lord your God with all your heart, and with all your soul, and with all your mind, and with all your strength. The second is this: Love your neighbor as yourself. There is no greater commandment than these." All their major family decisions are based on whether or not they're expressing love to God or to their fellow man. The statements concerning heart, soul, mind and strength encompass every area of possible priorities or decisions.

Another Family Mission Statement states, "We are a family who values relationships. We value family, friends and our community. We value the quality of our inner lives through personal growth, spiritual insight and character development. We value education and the pursuit of wisdom. We value time spent helping others. We value honesty, commitment and kindness. We value each member of our family and each member of society. We value and respect the differences between us. We value laughter. We value joy. We value love. We value life."

Values and Topics

The following is a list of possible topics you may want to cover in some form on your Personal Priority List and/or Family Mission Statement. These topics are given in no particular order. Don't feel that your family needs to include each and every topic on this list in your statement. Remember, this is a list of your top priorities in life. If you find it difficult to narrow down your focus, try to limit yourself to no more than ten topics on your list.

Family	Community
Loyalty	Hobbies
Spirituality	Responsibility
Education	Compassion
Friendship	Faith

Courage	Moral Sense
Attitudes	Outdoor activities
Justice	Extended family
Gratitude	Career
Environment	Perseverance
Contentment	Honesty
Love	Entertainment
Fun	Creativity
Nurturing	Service
Intimacy	Empathy
Connectedness	Time Commitments

Now that it's done...

After a statement has been decided upon, your family can then decide as a group what to do with your statement. While the possible uses for the statement are varied, it's important to make sure it's not hidden away in a box or file somewhere and never glanced at again. That would defeat the whole purpose.

The Family Mission Statement can be printed onto small cards for each member to carry in their wallets as a reminder of the importance of their family and the values they're attempting to live out in their lives. The Mission Statement can also be done in calligraphy or painted, and then displayed in a frame in a prominent spot in the house. It can be read aloud in the group as a way to start regular family meetings, or as a brief opening word before a meal. Make your Family Mission Statement something to be proud of—make it beautiful, a work of art. If it's displayed in a public spot in your home, it can even become a valuable conversation starter with visitors and extended family members.

Remember, the purpose of the Family Mission Statement is to provide a framework for identifying priorities in your life. As you make decisions in light of your priorities, you'll find a clearer focus to your life and find that life takes on a new simplicity.

A Simple Choice

Part Two
The Path to
Financial Freedom

CHAPTER SIX

🍂 Solving Payment Problems 🍂

"All of us who are intimately familiar with overspending know that it is very easy to five-and-ten dollar ourselves into oblivion. The good news is that you can five-and-ten dollar yourself right back to financial health, too." —Mary Hunt, *The Complete Cheapskate*

Now that we've taken steps to find focus for our lives by identifying our personal priorities, it's time to get down to some of the practical solutions for some of the difficult situations people often face in their day to day lives. The first step is taking care of our general financial health.

What can you do if you're having trouble paying your bills?

First, it's time to take serious stock of your finances. I'd like to suggest you follow these next steps so you'll know exactly where you stand financially. It won't be an educated guess, you'll know where your finances stand with certainty. Here are the steps:

1. Using your credit statements, make a complete list of everyone you owe money to—both individuals and companies.

2. Write down the total amount owed on all your debts and add the numbers together to find your total debt load.

3. Now, add up the total amount of payments you need to make each month.

4. Add together all the income you're certain you'll be receiving for the month.

5. Subtract from your total income, the absolute bare essentials—rent or house payment, food and utilities.

If you find that you don't have enough money left to make your minimum credit payments, it's time for some serious work on your financial condition.

This might seem like common sense, but the first step to getting out of debt is admitting you have a problem. Often people get behind in their payments or get in over their heads but find it hard to admit they've made a mistake and need to reorganize their thinking and their spending. It's much easier to get into debt than it is to get out, so it's sometimes difficult to step out onto a path that's going to be challenging. If you've identified a problem in the area of personal debt, you'll need to set about remedying the situation. Here are easy steps to regaining financial control.

Ten Simple Steps to Conquer Debt

1) Seek help. If you're not sure how to proceed, or you're feeling too overwhelmed to act for yourself, call a non-profit credit counseling program for advice and assistance in working with your creditors to set up a repayment plan. Consumer Credit Counseling Service has offices throughout the United States. Call 1-800-388-CCCS, 24 hours a day, for an office near you. You can also find information about debt problems from your local church, library or bank. If you have Internet access, look for information on-line as well.

2) Contact your creditors as soon as you're aware you won't be able to make a payment. Creditors are more likely to work with you if they're

contacted before the payment is actually overdue. Debt collectors are trained to solve payment problems, so don't be afraid to be honest with them about your financial situation. Stay calm. If you commit to paying the bill by a certain date, be sure you follow through on that commitment. The creditor won't be likely to work with you again if you don't keep your payment promises. If you can't make your minimum monthly payments, write to each creditor individually and see if you can work out smaller regular monthly bills. Be sure to explain to them why you fell behind in your bills, your current income, your other financial obligations and the exact amount you can pay them each month. I've included at the end of this chapter a sample letter to creditors you can alter to describe your personal circumstances.

3) Cut up all credit cards and send them back to the issuing companies immediately. Officially close all credit accounts by writing a letter to the company and having the primary cardholder sign the letter. The temptation when you start seeing lower balances on your accounts could lead you to charge the credit limits right back up again if the accounts remain open. Don't take out anymore loans or open any new credit accounts until back bills are paid in full.

4) Set a frugal budget and live within it. It's often easier to decrease spending than increase income. Don't make any purchases above and beyond the absolute basics until you've made some headway in catching up on your back bills. Consider selling assets to find more money for your debt repayment. Simple things, like holding a large garage sale can sometimes generate enough money to help pay an immediate bill or two.

5) Prioritize debts. Mortgages, child support and any debt that has gone to a collection agency is a priority. After you've identified the first priority debts, look for the credit companies that are charging you the most interest.

6) Pay each creditor something, no matter how small the amount. It will show good faith on your part as you try to negotiate payment arrangements.

7) Track personal spending to identify the holes where your money is draining out. Keep a detailed record for one month of every expenditure, no matter how insignificant. Little expenses on a regular basis add up quickly. Carry a small notebook with you and write down every single purchase. Now you'll know where your money's going.

8) Plug up any holes discovered from the spending record.

9) Plan ahead for annual expenses (i.e.: insurance, car licenses, medical deductibles, etc.).

10) Set long term financial goals and make all current financial decisions with your future well-being in mind. Keep the end result in mind—debt-free living!

Letter to Creditors

The letter on the following page is one you can customize to suit your needs. It helps to explain to creditors your exact situation and your payment options. Be sure to fill in the blanks and all [brackets] with appropriate information about your situation.

Your street address
Your city, state, ZIP
Date letter written

Company X
Street Address
Their city, state, ZIP

Re: Account Number: [enter your account number for this company here]

Dear Sir or Madam:
I'm writing to inform you I'm currently experiencing financial difficulties. Due to [unforeseen medical bills, a recent divorce, a brief period of unemployment, wage reduction, etc.], I am having trouble making my minimum monthly payments. I hope to arrange an acceptable debt-repayment plan with your company. I have prepared a frugal budget for myself, and have developed a debt-repayment plan that I am proposing to each of my creditors.

I owe _____ [number of] creditors more than $_____ , and my total asset value is less than $_____. My personal assets consist of [a car with blue-book value of $_____, home furnishing worth $_____, clothing, etc.]. My take home pay each month is $_____. After subtracting my basic living expenses, I have $_____ left for debt repayment.

I would like to ask you to accept partial payment of $_____ per month for _____ months until my debt to you is repaid in full. I will send you the first payment on [month, day, year].

Sincerely,

Your Name

CHAPTER SEVEN

❧ Spending Plans ❧

"Happiness is making the most of what you have."
—Rosamunde Pilcher

Probably the greatest single help to our family's financial situation has been establishing a budget. Now don't start hyperventilating and tune me out. I realize the B-word (Budget!) sometimes does strange things to people. If the word "budget" makes you sweat and turn purple, try substituting the phrase "spending plan." For some reason a Spending Plan is psychologically less threatening to many people than a b-b-b-b-b-budget.

The spending plan our family implemented is known as The Envelope System. It's easy, painless and it works. This simple plan did more to turn around our financial picture than any other single change we've made in our spending habits.

First, we figured out how much money we needed each month for the different expense categories (food, clothing, gasoline, bus fare, coffee at work, etc.) and then placed that amount of cash (yes, the green paper stuff!) into separately labeled envelopes. We then had a concrete visual aid to show exactly how much money we had left to spend in each category. We clearly saw how borrowing money from one envelope left less money in the other category. With this system, once the money's gone from one category, it's gone!

The envelope system is perfect for people who tend to think if there's a positive balance in the checkbook, they can keep writing checks. My husband and I learned this simple budgeting trick from the old Marlo Thomas television show, "That Girl."

checks. My husband and I learned this simple budgeting trick from the old Marlo Thomas television show, "That Girl."

There's no magic formula to living within your means, whatever those means might be. Whether you're a struggling one income family, a single working mother, or a double income family with mounting consumer debt, we can all use a good dose of reality in the financial area of our lives.

I've known people living beneath the poverty line who never go into debt and never have outstanding bills. I've also known families living in the grandest homes in town struggling to stay afloat each month due to overspending. Take it from someone who knows firsthand; it's easy to get into debt but much harder to dig your way back out. The old cliché is true: the only way to get out of debt is to stop going into debt! The envelope system could be just the tool you need to be able to live within your means without adding more debt to your life.

There are many other ways to trim costs and learn to control your finances instead of having them control you. In this chapter we'll look at some realistic ideas that you can implement.

General Budget Guidelines

I'm frequently asked how much money people should be spending on various categories. While many of these amounts vary depending on a family's income, goals or lifestyle, I believe the following can give a rough estimate for budgeting expenses.

Some of these categories are extremely flexible. For example, a family with a high income isn't going to be spending 25% of their income on food, while some low income families will be hard pressed to even spend the minimum 15% on the same budget item. These numbers are strictly rough guidelines and not a definite plan that anyone has to follow to make their budget work. Use this as a springboard for creating percentages that work within your lifestyle.

CATEGORY	PERCENTAGE
Housing	30-35%

(rent/mortgage, taxes, insurance, utilities, telephone, garbage, repairs, furnishings, supplies)

Food	15-25%

(groceries, snacks, beverages)

Transportation	5-10%

(car loans, gas, oil, repairs, license renewal, bus fare)

Clothing	2-10%

(purchases, laundry, repairs, dry cleaning)

Medical	5-8%

(insurance, deductibles, prescriptions, glasses/contacts, over-the-counter medications)

Insurance	2-8%

(life, auto)

Education	1-2%

(home schooling families, those with day care or baby-sitter expenses and those who use private schools will spend more)

Credit cards	0-10%

(the lower, the better!)

Savings	2-10%

(even a tiny amount regularly is better than nothing)

Recreation	2-10%

(entertainment, sports, cable TV, dining out, books, newspapers, magazines, vacations)

Contributions	5-10%

(church, charities)

Other categories that your family might have in addition to the above include: child care, income tax payments, haircuts, cosmetics, club or union dues, pets, occupational tools.

Money is a Tool

It is important to remember that money is a tool. Like other tools, it needs to be maintained properly and taken care of. It's also meant to be used—but used appropriately. You wouldn't use a hammer to change a tire on your car. Likewise, you don't want to use money for a purpose that it's not intended.

A few examples of inappropriate uses of the money tool are: trying to buy love, attempting to purchase personal significance and looking to buy contentment. Love, personal significance and attitudes are attributes that money can't buy—but many of us try, don't we? Since fulfilling these needs is an important part of everyone's life, it's a wise decision to choose to invest your time and personal effort into these areas of life, rather than just throwing money at them. The money tool just won't do the job properly—in the same way that a hammer won't effectively change your car's tire.

A tool used correctly can be a tremendous help, though. Hammering a nail with a hammer rather than a tire iron is a successful expenditure of effort. Examples of proper uses of money include: spending money to help others, educating your children, starting your own business or meeting the daily needs of your family. Often I see people so caught up in the idea of saving money, that it changes from an attitude of careful stewardship into an attitude of greed and hoarding. When someone's children or grandchildren are hungry and the people have literally millions of dollars sitting in the bank gathering dust, they're not using their money "tool" properly.

CHAPTER EIGHT

🍂 Contentment 🍂

"I have learned to be content whatever the circumstances. I know what
it is to be in need, and I know what it is to have plenty. I have learned
the secret of being content in any and every situation, whether well-fed
or hungry, whether living in plenty or in want." Philippians 4:11-13

Do you ever struggle with feeling discontent? One day someone wrote
to me and said they enjoyed spending money to pamper themselves, so
they were looking for inexpensive luxury ideas. I did have a few suggestions, but I've found over the past several years that my idea of what
constitutes a luxury has changed greatly.

When my family started on a drastic debt-repayment plan, we had
no extra money for anything but the absolute barest necessities for
almost five years. I couldn't even shop at thrift stores for clothes—even
that would've been too expensive for our severely limited budget. We
learned to make things ourselves, accept hand-me-downs from friends,
make do with what we had or do without. It was either live like that or
be forced into a complete Chapter Seven Bankruptcy filing by our impa-
tient and increasingly nasty creditors. We chose to do what needed to be
done, no matter how difficult it might be temporarily, in order to pay
off our creditors—mainly huge hospital bills from premature babies.

One of the first things I noticed when we started our debt repayment plan was the discontent that seemed to overtake me almost constantly. Continual discontent was breeding an attitude in my life that
made it difficult to appreciate what I had and to find joy in my life. I
started praying I would discover where this discontent was coming from

so I could overcome it once and for all and put it to rest. Well, it turned out for me the main Contentment Robbers in my life at that time were:

1) MAIL ORDER CATALOGS. The beautiful items in these catalogs were a constant reminder of all the wonderful things I couldn't have anymore—I overcame this particular Contentment Robber by tossing all catalogs into the recycling bin as soon as they arrived without even glancing at them. Even the colorful covers were enough to start discontent brewing in my heart.

2) SHOPPING MALLS. I hadn't realized how much recreational shopping breeds discontent. So often I'd see something I suddenly needed, when in reality I didn't even know the item existed until I saw it on a recreational shopping trip. A woman from Vermont writes, "I sometimes feel discontent because I'm a self-diagnosed impulse buyer. It's still very hard for me to go shopping alone. But I have a great circle of friends and family who support me tremendously when I'm in the mall with them." Like this woman, I too felt a great deal of temptation to buy when I was in a mall. I started avoiding malls at all costs unless I had something specific I needed to buy—and even then I only went in for what was on my list and then I hurried right back out before I got distracted by some new housewares store (my personal weakness).

3) COMMERCIAL TELEVISION. Seeing all the latest and the greatest clothes, toys and gadgets constantly paraded before my eyes bred continual discontent in my life. I turned off the television except to watch the evening news, videos from the library, or Public Broadcasting specials with my kids. I've never watched shopping channels on television, but I suspect they're probably Contentment Robbers for some people. Also, certain shopping areas on the Internet may serve as Contentment Robbers.

4) WOMEN'S MAGAZINES. I didn't have many magazine subscriptions, but the pages of the ones I did receive showed perfect homes, beautiful clothes, pampering toiletries, etc., which caused me to suffer from what I

believe is a form of lust. I wanted those things so badly. I quit buying these magazines except for those that weren't littered with advertising.

5) BARGAIN STORES. Even going to thrift stores and garage sales can breed discontent—and also turn into a continuing temptation to overspend. Something I personally needed to realize was that spending money on a great bargain was still spending money! A woman in North Carolina writes, "as a shop-o-holic, it's been very hard not to spend money on clothes and household items. I used to take pride in the bargains I would find and feel like I'd accomplished a lot in a successful shopping trip. Now I take pride in every day that I don't spend any money at all—not even on a bargain."

6) COMPARISON WITH OTHERS. This was probably the most important aspect of contentment that I needed to learn. The Bible says that comparing ourselves among ourselves is not wise. Looking longingly at the often extravagant purchases many people around me were able to make was a great hindrance to my personal contentment. I was disregarding the fact that many of these people were able to buy so much because they were using credit cards and getting further and further in debt. I needed to keep my eyes firmly on my own situation and not worry about what was happening with others. Did I really believe that a meaningful life consisted of more than just the outward trappings of wealth? If so, then I needed to remind myself of that fact daily.

I also realized that many of those wealthy friends were discontent with their lives, which is what was leading them to buy more and more things to try and fill an internal void. I came to understand that if I could learn to be content when I was in need, I could also be content if I ever found myself in a position of plenty. A teacher in California writes, "when I made a lot of money, I was always discontent. If I had a new stereo, I needed a newer one with more features. If I had trendy clothes, I had to buy more as soon as the styles changed. There was always something newer and bigger and better that I needed. I spent all my energy acquiring stuff that never made me happy. Since I don't buy into this lifestyle anymore, I have more than enough money to own a good pair of hiking boots and backpack, take a guided kayaking tour down the river of my choice, treat my three-year-old niece to a day in the park and dinner for just the two of us, or jump on an airplane to visit my grandparents who live in another state. It all goes back to spending energy and money only on those things that are vitally important to me, and not worrying about what everyone else is doing."

Probably the biggest surprise of all to me was that the longer I practiced frugal living and continued to read books on the topic, I found I was finding more and more satisfaction in the simpler pursuits I was now practicing. Simplicity was becoming far more fulfilling than all the shopping and personal luxury items which I'd previously considered such a treat.

A homemaker in California writes, "there is a great feeling of accomplishment that comes from getting by on less money, from making things yourself and doing without unnecessary things. Even though we're barely paying the bills, we're much happier than we were when money was plentiful. The peace and tranquility that we've gained has far exceeded our expectations, and shown us that we can be happy without all the material things society says we have to have to be happy."

We're no longer in debt, but money is still tight. For a single income family of five, money is always tight. But I'm not discontent anymore. I have great satisfaction knowing that our debts are paid in full—paying off our debts is one of our greatest luxuries in and of itself.

Through the process of getting our finances in order, I've gained a new appreciation for the beauty and joy of life's simpler pleasures. Shopping and acquiring new stuff holds little appeal to me anymore. Now I would much rather spend a day hiking in nature and picnicking in a meadow with my kids, than spend an expensive afternoon sauntering around the mall, eating designer cinnamon rolls and sipping almond cappuccinos.

CHAPTER NINE

One Income Living
🍂 in a Two Income World 🍂

"A man may be very industrious, and yet not spend his time well. There is no more fatal blunderer than he who consumes the greater part of life getting his living." —Henry David Thoreau

I often receive notes from people interested in simplifying their lives so they can be home full-time with their children. It seems to be a common desire in many families, but it often seems so far out of reach in what has been frequently described as a two income economy.

I hear it all the time: "It must be nice making so much money you can be home with your kids. We could never afford to do that."

What people don't know is that our family of five has lived for years on a salary that could easily qualify for several low-income programs. That is okay with me. My husband and I have voluntarily, and quite happily, chosen this frugal lifestyle. But it's funny to hear the misconceptions others have about our finances.

The assumption seems to be, if you're home with your children full-time you must be rolling in piles of money. Common urban folklore unsettles us with the idea that it will cost around three hundred thousand dollars to raise each child to adulthood. According to those figures, it would cost nearly a million dollars to raise our three children! Gulp . . . .

Maybe the numbers are accurate if I bought my children's clothing exclusively at upscale specialty stores, sent them to ultra-expensive private schools, and outfitted their rooms with the latest audio/visual equipment and top-of-the-line designer crib ensembles.

The reality in our neighborhood is drastically different. Nearly every family on our block made the conscious decision, at least for a time, to make the necessary sacrifices so that one parent can be home with their children.

I hope you won't think when reading this that we've all dropped out of life and taken up an existence of soap operas and bon-bons. Far from it. Many of the women have cottage industries or attend college. Some do consulting work to stay abreast of their professions. A neighbor stays home with her children, actively pursuing the dream of a writing career.

Even with the occasional part-time income, the families on our street don't make the money that statistics claim will be needed to adequately raise our kids.

But raise them successfully, we will!

The Secret

So, what's the secret to "one income living in a two income world" ? Actually, there are several easy tricks:

1) WATCH YOUR PURCHASES. Watch your purchases, even small ones, carefully. If you're cautious with your pennies, the dollars will take care of themselves. Little expenses add up quickly if they're done on a regular basis.

Groceries are one of the few fairly flexible expense categories in most families. Learn tricks for saving money by careful meal planning and using up leftovers. Investigate the concept of cooking for the freezer (i.e. Frozen Assets). Learn to buy in bulk and take advantage of lower prices by planning your menus around the grocery sale flyers in the newspaper.

2) LIVE WITHIN YOUR MEANS. Vow to live within your means. This is easier said than done, but it can be done—I'm living proof. The first step toward ensuring that your outgo doesn't exceed your income is establishing a budget. Whether it's an actual written budget, or the Envelope System recommended earlier, you'll need to figure out how much money you need each month for the different categories. The Envelope System is a great method for people who tend to think that as long as there's a positive balance in the checkbook, they can keep on writing checks.

3) GET OUT OF DEBT. Get out of debt—and stay out! Recently it's become standard that over one million personal bankruptcies are filed each year in the United States. The majority of these are the result of poorly managed consumer debt. If you have large amounts of personal debt, or you're starting to feel in bondage to your creditors, carefully read the chapters on debt in this book. For more in-depth personal help, consider contacting a credit counselor or financial planner. Consumer Credit Counseling Service (CCCS) offers free financial advice, debt counseling and they can work with your creditors to arrange easier payment plans. Call 1-800-388-CCCS for the office near you.

4) IDENTIFY PRIORITIES. Identify your personal priorities. No one can set your family's priorities for you. But if you don't take the time to think them through, articulate them clearly and live them out, you may find you've lived a life that isn't a true reflection of your inner desires and motivations.

Clarify your personal definition of success and meaningfulness by writing out a brief Mission Statement for your family and/or personal life. Then evaluate every purchase and activity in light of your personal life mission.

If having time for community involvement is an important priority, can you pare back the nonessential activities to allow room for volunteering and service? Watching evening television might be a relaxing pastime, but is it adding anything to your community's quality of life?

If staying home with your children is a top priority, are you willing to do whatever it takes to make it happen? It's not a crime to shop at thrift stores for your family's wardrobe essentials, and your children won't hate you if you don't take them to Hawaii every year. These are obviously extreme examples, but I think you get the point.

5) A SUPPORT NETWORK. Establish a support network of friends in similar financial circumstances. If money is tight, every decision can become a financial one. It helps to have friends who understand personally the difficulties you sometimes face and that can offer support for the choices you're making.

6) RESOURCES. Tap into the many resources available for frugality and simple living. There are newsletters, books, web-sites and even local study groups that can inspire you, and offer practical ideas for living within your means. See the resources section of this book for specific resources.

What it Takes

It doesn't take a salary the size of Bill Gates' to live on one income. But it does take careful planning, focused priorities and a nonnegotiable commitment to stay out of debt. There are often some sacrifices involved, but if your heart's desire is to be home with your children, the rewards of staying true to your convictions will far outweigh any losses you might experience.

Our family faced these decisions many years ago. We followed our dream and we'll never regret it. For years, I've driven a used, rusty station wagon with nearly 300,000 miles on it. Laugh if you must when I drive by, but we don't make car payments and our yearly license fees and insurance premiums are minimal. Driving used cars is just one of the many choices we've made that allow me to be home each day with our young children.

Am I making sacrifices? Maybe. At least in the eyes of some people.

But for me, the real sacrifice would be giving up the joys I share each day with my three children—laughing together, growing and learning side by side, being available to others in need—these are joys that I can never recapture if I miss this opportunity now.

Carpe diem. Seize the day.

By making a few not-so difficult financial decisions, we've been able to reach our dream of living on one income in a two income world. If you share that dream, I believe you can make it happen as well. It can be difficult at times, but the benefits of making it work are out of this world!

Part Three
🍂 The Simplified Kitchen 🍂

CHAPTER TEN

An Introduction to Frozen Assets

"If the mealtime is meaningful and fun and well prepared, the family table becomes more of an altar than an eating counter." –Stephen R. Covey, *The Seven Habits of Highly Effective Families*

One of the most important areas of daily life that often needs to be simplified is meal preparation. The five o'clock dinner hour can cause more stress than any other time of the day for many families. Parents are just getting home from work, everyone's hungry, the kids are tired and now you have to cook? Sometimes it's just easier to swing through the drive-thru for the third time this week rather than think about and prepare another family meal during this harried time of day. One of the most helpful ways I've found for saving time, money and sanity in the kitchen is cooking meals ahead and storing them in the freezer for use later. Whether you choose to cook a couple days worth of meals ahead, or several weeks, having a homemade dinner on the table in fifteen minutes from start to finish could be the answer to many families' dinner time blues.

Following the premature birth of our first child, a group of ladies from church filled our freezer with two weeks of frozen meals. Between frequent visits to the I.C.U. Nursery and the normal stresses of starting a family, those meals in the freezer were a lifesaver. This was my introduction to the idea of freezing meals ahead. Since then, I've applied this concept to our regular family meals. I save substantial time, effort and money in the process.

Some cookbooks refer to this as "investment" cooking. Often I'll cook one day each month and have 30+ main dinner meals tucked away in my freezer, ready to thaw and heat for a month's worth of easy meals. By applying these methods to my own inexpensive recipes, I've been able to save money by purchasing in bulk. This method also cuts down on those quick (and very expensive!) trips through the local drive-thru when I'm rushing the kids to T- Ball practice or an evening meeting. I call my personal method of cooking ahead Frozen Assets, and have written a book with that title that gives detailed instructions on how to benefit fully from this idea. (*Frozen Assets: how to cook for a day and eat for a month,* Champion Press, 1999.)

If you're thinking, "I could never do this. I only have a small fridge top freezer," don't tune me out. When I first started cooking ahead, I only had the small freezer attached to the refrigerator. By packaging meals in plastic freezer bags and freezing the bags flat, I was able to store an entire month's worth of Frozen Assets in my small freezer.

An easy way to start building up a supply of Frozen Assets is by doubling or tripling recipes as you prepare them during the week. If you're making lasagna, prepare three: one for eating tonight and two for the freezer. Just one week of tripling recipes will give you a stockpile in your freezer of two weeks of meals with virtually no extra effort.

Andrea, the mother of a two-year-old and seven months pregnant with twins, started investment cooking. Realizing her hands would soon be full during those busy postpartum days, she said, "I don't have the stamina to devote an entire day to standing on my feet cooking, unless I want to send myself into labor right now! So, I'm going to triple recipes of easy meals every night until the babies arrive. I know the extra work now will pay off when I find myself less harried later."

No matter who you are, how big your family or what your lifestyle, whether you're a single working parent or a mother at home fulltime with your children, investment cooking has something to offer everyone.

Frozen Assets could be the answer you've been looking for:

Save $$$ on your food budget.

Save time in the kitchen each day.

Increase the outreach opportunities frozen meals can provide (meals for the sick, the young mom on bedrest, a grieving family, etc.).

Small Freezer Syndrome

One of the most common concerns I hear about preparing meals for the freezer is: "I only have the small freezer above my refrigerator—how can I still do a full month of cooking ahead?"

For someone with only a fridge-top freezer, I usually recommend starting with twice-a-month cooking, or just doubling and tripling recipes as you go about your regular cooking during the week. As you get used to the method and learn ways to efficiently pack your freezer, you may eventually be able to store the entire month's worth of dinner entrees in your fridge-top freezer. When I first began cooking ahead, we only had a small refrigerator freezer. It was almost two years before I had a second larger freezer to store my Frozen Assets—so it can be done. It just takes careful planning.

Before you do a big day of freezer meal cooking, clear out all the various nonessentials from your freezer. Wait until the freezer empties later in the month before stocking up on frozen bread, ice cream, etc.

To save space, use heavy-duty freezer bags for storing most of your frozen meals, rather than baking dishes or disposable foil pans. When using freezer bags, remove all excess air (suck the air out with a straw or press the air gently out of the bag from the top of the food toward the opening of the bag), freeze the bags flat and then pack them in the freezer carefully. To prevent a possible landslide of stacked freezer meals, store your frozen bags of food standing on edge—much as you'd stack old-fashioned record albums.

Another way to conserve freezer space is by preparing meals of sauces to pour over pasta or rice. Prepare the pasta or rice on serving day so it doesn't take up precious space in your freezer.

If you're in the market for a separate freezer but can't afford to buy a new one, don't despair. Ask friends, relatives and neighbors to keep an eye out for people moving out of state or updating their kitchens. I've known many people who've found perfectly good freezers for free just by making a few phone calls. Check your local newspaper's classified ads under Appliances, and also look through the garage sale listings for any that are selling appliances. Also, keep a look out at yard sales, tag sales, appliance repair stores and auctions of dented white goods.

Top Ten Questions and Answers

I've been teaching about cooking ahead for several years and I've noticed that the same questions are asked over and over again by audiences everywhere. The following are the most frequently asked questions (other than the too-small-freezer question).

1) HOW DO I COOK FOR AN ENTIRE DAY WITH TWO TODDLERS UNDERFOOT? Some possibilities: cook with a friend and then trade off child care and cooking duty; have your spouse take the children out for the day; enlist a friend or neighbor to watch your kids on cooking day and offer to watch hers in return; let the kids spend the day with grandparents; barter some frozen home-cooked meals in exchange for a few hours of baby-sitting.

2) HOW DO I KNOW WHAT WILL FREEZE WELL AND WHAT WON'T? If you're unsure, freeze a small amount as a test. Greasy foods just get greasier when frozen. Foods that do not freeze well or change in the freezer: cake icings made with egg whites; cream fillings and soft frostings; pies made with custard or cream fillings; cooked egg white; fried foods tend to become soggy; soft cheese (such as cream cheese) can become watery; mayonnaise separates (use salad dressing instead); sour cream; potatoes cooked in soups and stews become mushy and may darken; gravies and other fat-based sauces may separate and need to be recombined by

stirring or processing in the blender; thickened sauces may need thinning after freezing; seasonings such as onions, herbs and flavorings used in recipes can change during freezing; vegetables, pastas and grains used in cooked recipes usually are softer after freezing and re-heating (under-cook before freezing or add when dish is reheated); heavy cream can be frozen if used for cooking, but will not whip; some yogurts may suffer texture changes; raw vegetables lose their crispness but can be used for cooking, stews, etc.; some cheeses change texture in the freezer.

3) WHAT CAN I USE FOR FREEZER CONTAINERS? Plastic freezer boxes with lids; ceramic, glass and metal bake-ware; heavy-duty freezer bags. Be sure to check garage sales and thrift stores for these items. A recommendation from a long time freezer-meal cook in San Diego, CA.: "I recommend rectangular things for storage. You'll get more into your freezer. If you use round things, space is lost between them. Some suggestions are: line baking pans with heavy duty aluminum foil, mold to corners carefully, leaving extra to fold over and seal it shut. Add your meal, cook if neces-sary. Let cool. If cooking is not necessary, fold over and seal the foil. Label and date. Put the baking dish into the freezer. When the meal is frozen, remove frozen meal from baking dish and return package to freezer. Almost any plastic food container is safe for freezing food in, but don't use them in the microwave unless they say they are okay for that purpose. I know many a once-a-month cook who has lots of Pyrex™ dishes they buy at yard sales or thrift shops and they use these, well wrapped, to store their meals in the freezer."

4) IF I DO A COMPLETE 30 MEAL COOKING SESSION, WILL IT COST A LOT FOR THE INITIAL INVESTMENT IN A FULL MONTH'S WORTH OF FOOD? It depends on how elaborate your meals and how much you cook from scratch. Convenience foods are much more expensive than their homemade counterparts. It might cost a bit more the first time, but because you'll be purchasing some items in bulk, the cost could actually be quite a bit less than you'd expect. If coming up with the initial money for a com-plete month of meals is difficult, start out with twice-a-month cooking.

5) My kitchen is tiny. How can I handle a large amount of cooking in such a small space? Make extra counter space by turning off the gas stove and lighting burners as needed. Set up a card table in the living room. Use the kitchen or dining room table for food prep, too. If the washer and dryer are handy to the kitchen, you can use them as additional countertops. Organize yourself by thinking through your cooking steps ahead of time. Assemble like recipes together. Do all chicken, then beef, then beans, etc.

6) How do I label things? What sort of labels, pens, etc., do I need to use? Inexpensive labels applied to the foil before freezing will usually work fine. If you use freezer paper, you can write directly on it with a grease pencil. You can use a Sharpie brand permanent marker directly on the freezer bag or foil. Write the name of the meal, date frozen, reheating directions and any other unusual instructions (i.e. sprinkle with grated cheese before baking). If you double bag items in freezer bags, you can slip a note card with the labeling instructions between the two bags. Then you can reuse the label and outer bag again and again.

7) I love this idea, but I don't have a full day available for a big cooking session. Are there other ways of cooking ahead? You can cook 3 or 4 meals at a time rather than a whole month's worth. Also, doubling and tripling recipes will help you quickly build up a stock of frozen meals. It really doesn't take more time to make a large pot of spaghetti for freezing extras, than it does to make a single meal's worth of sauce.

8) Are all the meals casseroles or pasta-with-sauce recipes? You can freeze almost anything: soups, casseroles, sandwiches, meals to serve over rice, chicken dishes, meatloaf, etc.

9) I'm a vegetarian...Any special tips? There shouldn't be any problem adapting this method to vegetarian menus. Prepare a recipe and try freezing a single portion before you attempt a larger batch of freezer

meals (this tip applies to any recipe you haven't tried in the freezer). You can substitute TVP (texturized vegetable protein) in many recipes calling for ground meats. Tofu, cooked beans and bean-based meals usually freeze well.

10) ARE THERE SPECIAL POTS AND PANS, UTENSILS OR APPLIANCES I SHOULD HAVE ON HAND TO MAKE A BIG COOKING DAY GO EASILY? The following are nice to have on a big cooking day: a food processor for chopping large quantities of onions, celery, etc.; good quality sharp knives; several large heavy stock pots; long handled spoons for stirring and mixing; an electric can opener; a crockpot; a salad shooter works well for grating large amounts of cheese. If you're cooking ahead breakfast items, you might want a waffle iron to make homemade frozen waffles (much tastier than the ones you buy from the freezer case). You don't necessarily need to purchase all of these items. I borrow my neighbor's large stock pot and waffle iron each cooking day.

Cooking with a Friend

Does the thought of preparing 30+ meals by yourself sound like a lonely way to spend the day? Consider sharing the job with a friend. Not only is it fun, you can also share cooking utensils, pots and pans, recipes and cooking know-how.

You'll need to choose someone with similarities in family size, appetites and taste preferences. Special dietary requirements also need to be taken into consideration. Choosing a partner who is cooking for the same size family really helps when it comes time to divide the meals—simply split everything fifty/fifty. But most importantly, you need to choose someone you enjoy spending time with—it's a much better idea to choose your best friend rather than the best cook you know (unless the best cook is also someone you love to be with for hours on end).

It might not be as difficult as you think, to agree on which meals to prepare. Get together with your intended cooking partner and each of you bring a list of ten to twelve of your family's favorite everyday meals. If you plan on tripling recipes as you prepare them, you'll only need to agree on ten recipes total for a full 30 days of meals.

It helps if you divide the various duties beforehand—maybe one of you can do the shopping one month while the other takes care of baby-sitting duties; and someone could prepare chicken meals while the other prepares ground beef recipes.

One potential difficulty of cooking with someone else is a lack of freezer space during cooking day. You might want to plan on cooking at the home of whoever has the most available freezer space. Also, have several picnic coolers handy for transporting frozen meals to your home.

Freezer Meal Potluck

If you know a group of people experienced in freezer-meal cooking, you can arrange for a group meal exchange. This is sometimes referred to as a "freezer potluck." I'm referring to a method where everyone prepares their meals at home separately and then brings the freezer-meals to an "exchange meeting." It would be a bit more difficult logistically for a group cooking day where everyone joins together to cook in the same kitchen—although I've heard of that option being used for groups cooking in church or community center kitchens.

For example, if there are ten people in your cooking group, everyone would prepare ten family-sized portions of one recipe. Then the group would get together every so often to exchange fully frozen meals. This works much like a glorified Cookie Exchange. To discover meals that most people in the group would like, ask each group member to list their three family favorite meals or what they frequently serve to company. Then be sure to let everyone in the group vote on which recipe each person will prepare. For this to work, you really need to be in

100% agreement about the meals that are being prepared. This potluck technique works well for the people I know who have tried it—each family gets a variety of frozen meals without one person having to do all the cooking by themselves.

Lunches

Lunches at home can be prepared easily in advance. Smaller servings of your regular dinner items can be served for a lighter noon-time meal. Many items can be frozen and then included in brown bag lunches, as well.

SANDWICHES: These freeze well. Fillings that work for freezing include cooked meat, tuna, sliced cheese, cheese spreads, hard cooked egg yolks and nut butters. Use day old bread; spread bread lightly with butter or margarine to prevent fillings soaking into bread; mixing jelly, mayonnaise or salad dressing into the sandwich filling helps prevent soggy bread. Tomatoes and lettuce get limp when frozen, so add these after removing sandwich from freezer. Frozen sandwiches will thaw in lunch boxes in about three to four hours, staying fresh and cooling other foods in the lunch box at the same time.

QUICHE: For lunches, cooked quiche can be frozen in individually wrapped slices. Serve warm (heated in microwave) or cold.

SOUP: Homemade soups can be frozen easily in microwave-safe single-serving containers. Heat in microwave until thawed and hot.

DESSERTS: Cookies and cakes can be frozen in individual servings and then placed still frozen into the lunch bag.

All Purpose Ground Meat Mix

One of the easiest ways to save money on your family's grocery bill is by purchasing foods in bulk when they go on sale. When ground meat goes on sale, rather than just stocking up to store in the freezer "as is," many cooks find it helpful to prepare meat mixes for using later in their favorite family recipes.

By preparing this recipe for All-Purpose Ground Meat Mix, you'll be ready to fix any number of tasty ground meat recipes without needing to brown the meat, onions and spices each time you cook. Not only will this technique save you money, it saves time too.

The following recipe is from the book *Frozen Assets: How to Cook for a Day and Eat for a Month* by Deborah Taylor-Hough (Champion Press, ISBN: 1891400614).

ALL-PURPOSE GROUND MEAT MIX
(Makes about 12 cups)
This is a basic ground meat mix that can be used in many casseroles and recipes.

5 pounds ground meat (beef or turkey)
2 cups celery, chopped
1 clove garlic, minced
2 cups onion, chopped
1 cup green pepper, diced
½ teaspoon pepper
1 teaspoon salt (optional)

Brown meat in a large pot. Drain. Stir in celery, garlic, onion, green pepper, salt and pepper; cover and simmer about 10 minutes until vegetables are tender but not soft. You can use this mixture immediately during your cooking session or freeze in two-cup portions for later use.

SUGGESTED USES (be creative):

TACOS: Add one package taco seasoning to two cups All-Purpose Ground Meat Mix (follow package directions for amount of water). Freeze. To serve: thaw and heat taco mixture; prepare tacos as you would normally.

TACO POTATOES: Follow instructions for taco mixture (above), but serve the mixture over baked potatoes instead of tortillas or taco shells. Top with grated cheese, diced tomatoes, sour cream, sliced green onions, sliced black olives and salsa.

EASY TACO SALADS: Follow instructions for taco mixture; place a layer of corn chips or tortilla chips on plate; spoon taco mixture over chips; add layer of shredded lettuce; add diced tomatoes, sliced green onions, sliced black olives, sour cream and salsa.

SLOPPY JOES: In a large skillet, place two cups Ground Meat Mix, one (10 ¾ ounce) can tomato soup, two tablespoons brown sugar, and one teaspoon prepared mustard. Stir. Cover and simmer ten minutes. Serve ladled onto hamburger buns.

The All-Purpose Ground Meat Mix can also be used for: stuffed peppers, chili, spaghetti, and baked ziti. (Further recipes can be found in the *Frozen Assets* book. See the back of this book for ordering information.)

More Freezer Friendly Recipes

For a full list of recipes that work wonderfully in the freezer, please refer to my book *Frozen Assets: how to cook for a day and eat for a month*. This book contains techniques for adapting your favorite recipes to your own customized one month cooking plan. There are also several other cookbooks available with recipes for the freezer. Visit the cookbook section of your local bookstore or check your favorite online bookseller. I also maintain a web page with ideas for freezer cooking and other simplicity tips. A free newsletter that is sent via e-mail 24 times a year is also available at the site. Visit it at

http://members.aol.com/Dsimple/index.html

CHAPTER ELEVEN

🍃 Saving on Meal Expenses 🍃

"The discovery of a new dish does more for the happiness of the human race than the discovery of a star." –Jean Anthelme Brillat-Savarin

How much money do you spend on groceries for your family? $150 per week? $100? Believe it or not, it's relatively easy to spend as little as $50 per week on groceries for a family of five or six. Simplifying the family grocery bill can be challenging and requires a bit of time and effort to implement, but by following some of these suggestions, you won't only save money but your kids could start eating healthier meals than the ones that come in a children's meal box with a toy car.

When I first started investigating frugal food shopping, I was spending easily $600 per month on groceries for my family (more if you add toiletries and paper products into the total). After learning some tricks for shopping wisely and planning ahead, I've been able to reduce our family's food bill to as little as $50 per week (not including toiletries, etc.). I'm not always as diligent about this as I could be, so we sometimes spend more than this amount, but if I'm careful this is not a far flung dream but an easily achievable reality.

Breakfast

To save at breakfast, steer clear of the pretty and expensive pre-packaged dry cereals. Boxes of breakfast cereal might be easy, but they're usually more expensive. Save those expensive boxed cereals for an occasional treat rather than everyday breakfast fare. Instead, rely on less expensive homemade alternatives. Oatmeal is probably the least expensive breakfast item you can prepare, especially if you buy it in bulk or purchase store brands. Dress oatmeal up with raisins, brown sugar, cinnamon, bits of fruit, or whatever makes it special for your family. Rice, barley and other whole grains can be cooked and eaten like oatmeal for a change of pace. Or try a mixture of several different cooked grains. If your family is in the habit of having cereal, and there aren't any suitable substitutes, try using the generic brands. Many times a company will package the same product under a generic label. The cost difference of many items is in the packaging—not the products themselves. To avoid the look of generic for picky eaters, store the cereal in one of the airtight Rubbermaid™ cereal containers.

Other inexpensive breakfast ideas include: homemade muffins, pancakes, waffles, French toast, egg sandwiches and breakfast burritos. Many of these items can be made ahead of time and kept in the freezer for quick and simple breakfasts when your family's rushing out the door to work and school.

Buy breakfast juices as frozen concentrate—saving about half the cost of bottled juice. If you serve juice in small glasses rather than larger beverage glasses, it really makes the juice stretch.

Omelets are also an economical meal. They're a good source of protein and a great way to use up leftover meats, vegetables and cheeses.

Lunch

Keep lunches at home simple: sandwiches, soups, salads, fresh fruit, sliced cheese and crackers are all quick and easy choices. Lunch is also a good time to use up some of the week's leftovers.

Lunches away from home (at school or work) are often a difficult meal to save money on. The easiest secret is to avoid pre-packaged convenience foods. Sandwiches made from that old standby, peanut butter and jelly, are still a big hit with kids today. Also, lunch meats are often less expensive per pound if purchased at the deli counter rather than in prepackaged containers.

If you have access to a microwave at work, package up your dinner leftovers as a homemade TV dinner to reheat for lunch. Or freeze small portions of homemade lasagna or other freezer meals to heat at lunch.

Bring reusable thermos bottles filled with juice or milk instead of buying individual juice boxes.

For dessert, pack a slice of homemade cake or a brownie. Sometimes you can find cake mixes for as little as $0.25 per box. You can bake the cake ahead of time, slice into serving sizes, wrap individually, and then freeze. The frozen cake can go directly into the lunch box, keeping the other foods cool and defrosting easily by noon. You can also purchase single serving snacks and desserts at inexpensive bakery outlet stores for keeping in the freezer until needed.

When packing lunches for your children to take to school, pack your own gelatin, pudding, applesauce or fruit cup snacks in small plastic reusable containers.

Dinner

For busy families, it's often easier to swing by the local drive-thru restaurant, rather than worry about cooking a new meal every night. If this describes your dinner-time dilemma, keep ingredients on hand for several quick and easy meals. One of the best solutions is the freezer cooking method detailed in the previous chapter.

Consider instituting a 'bread and soup' night once a week. You can prepare homemade soup using leftover meats and vegetables collected in the freezer during the week. Bake a loaf of homemade bread and you're all set for a tasty, satisfying and inexpensive meal. If you cook a large pot of soup one night a week, you can make enough for lunches for a couple days during the week as well.

Occasionally serve breakfast for dinner. Even when prepared in a big way, breakfast is one of the most economical meals to make. At our house we rarely have time for a big breakfast of pancakes, eggs and bacon in the morning, so it's a special treat to have a meal like that for dinner now and then. Omelets also make a good dinner choice.

Consider serving dessert as an occasional special treat rather than an everyday occurrence. It's easier on the wallet and the waistline.

Making the Most of Leftovers

Leftovers...what do we do with them? I personally don't like keeping them in my refrigerator until a science project on mold develops, but sometimes it's hard to know what to use leftovers for without driving the family crazy. I don't care to hear another chorus of that all-too-familiar refrain, "What? Meatloaf . . . AGAIN?!"

Probably the most important step with leftovers is making sure to keep them safe. We're not saving money on our family budget if that frugal dinner of leftovers sends everyone to the hospital with food poisoning! To keep leftovers safe: 1) cover and refrigerate within two hours of a meal, 2) freeze to keep more than three days, and 3) thaw frozen leftovers in the refrigerator.

I try to plan one meal each week to use up leftovers. Often it's during a lunch time with just the kids and I, but sometimes there's enough food to feed the entire family. A complete meal of food that's been "found" in the refrigerator is like getting an extra meal each week for free. It's a good idea to try and change the way the leftover is served from one meal to the next. Rather than serving leftover fried chicken, you could take the meat off the bone and prepare cold chicken sandwiches for a change of pace.

Suggestions for Using Leftovers:

- Bread (loaf ends, slices starting to dry): bread pudding, French toast, meat loaf extender, croutons, stuffing, bread crumbs
- Egg (hard-cooked): casseroles, salads, sandwiches

- Fruit (fresh, canned or frozen): smoothies, milk shakes, gelatin desserts, cobblers, muffins, fruit bread, jam, freezer pops, sauces
- Meats, poultry, or fish (cooked): soups, stew, salad, quiche, enchiladas, stir fry, sandwiches, pot pies
- Potatoes (cooked): pot pie, salads, soups, stew
- Rice, pasta (cooked): casseroles, soups
- Vegetables (cooked): casseroles, quiche, salads, soups, over baked potato, pot pies

One of the things we do with our leftovers is to prepare a Party Tray meal. I'll take all the collected leftovers out of the fridge and freezer, reheat them and then divide the food items between each person's plate. Everyone gets a little dab of this and a little dab of that. There may be only a bite or two of each item, but after the plate is filled with bits and pieces from past meals, it takes on the look of a plate from a party buffet line. I usually add some sliced cheese and crackers plus a few cut up fresh veggies to complete the party theme.

My kids love this Party Tray meal idea. I hesitated for a long time to serve Party Tray to my husband, but one Saturday I threw together a Party Tray meal for lunch. I was so surprised—my husband thought it was a great idea and wanted to know why I didn't do this when he was around. So now Party Tray has become a regular meal event, enjoyed by the whole family.

One night each week we have a Soup and Bread night. I'll either bake a loaf of fresh bread, a bunch of hearty rolls or a big pan of cornbread. I keep a covered bucket in the freezer for storing assorted leftovers (meats, vegetables, rice, beans, etc.) to make soup. One woman told me she drew a lady's face on the soup bucket and called the lady the Freezer Fairy. Her children could hardly wait to feed their leftovers to the Freezer Fairy. Each week, they were excited to see what delicious soup she was going to make for their family. (By the way, the Freezer Fairy's magic doesn't work well on fish, so don't add leftover fish to your soup bucket in the freezer.)

CHAPTER TWELVE

🍂 Grocery Savings 🍂

"Go to the ant . . ., consider its ways and be wise..., it stores its provisions in summer and gathers its food at harvest."—Proverbs 6:6,8

Groceries are one of the few flexible items in a family budget, but it can sometimes be challenging to find creative ways to save on regular family food costs. Following are some simple tips for easy reductions in grocery expenses.

PLAN AHEAD. Whether you're planning on cooking your meals ahead of time to store in the freezer, or just planning your menu and shopping list for a month of regular shopping, planning ahead can simplify meal preparation during the month and also save money.

First, set your grocery budget and then make up the menus and grocery list to fit your budget—not the other way around. Decide what you can afford to spend and then don't go over that amount. You'd be surprised how creative you can be when you know you can only spend "this-much-and-no-more" at the store.

Take a few minutes to make a monthly menu and write down just what you need in the house for each meal. Go through the freezer and the cabinets, taking stock of what's already on hand. Then look at your calendar to see what the monthly activities are—for example, make note of any birthday dinners, evenings when everyone will be leaving the house for the evening, times you're eating at someone else's home or whatever events would effect your meal planning for the month.

Next, look at the sale flyers for your local grocery stores. To save the most money, plan your meals around what's on sale and what you already have on hand. If you plan to shop weekly, make up all your individual weekly grocery lists for the month ahead of time (write up the entire month of shopping lists in one day so all you'll need to do is run to the store when it's time to shop).

Write out your meal plan on a blank calendar page and hang it in an easily visible spot (on the refrigerator, on a family bulletin board, etc.). It takes time to make out the menu and grocery lists, but it saves even more time everyday—and causes much less stress—when the decision is already made about what's for supper that night.

SHOP WITH CASH. This is a surprisingly effective means of staying in budget. There seems to be a psychological phenomenon happening when you pay for something with a handful of twenty dollar bills rather than writing a check for the same amount. Writing a check somehow seems less concrete and makes it much easier to overspend. Subconsciously, it sometimes doesn't feel like you're spending real money.

Keeping your budgeted amount of money for groceries in a cash envelope is a strong visual reminder of exactly how much you have to spend on groceries. The temptation to spend a little extra and take the money from another budget category will be greatly reduced with this method.

KEEP A PRICE DIARY. Some people seem to be able to remember exactly what they've paid for every item they've purchased during the last two years. If you're not able to accomplish that particular trick (especially with all the small purchases made at the grocery store), a price diary will be a great help to your grocery budget.

Keep a list of all regularly purchased items (food, toiletries, paper products, etc.) in a small notebook, ideally something small enough to slip into your purse or pocket whenever you shop. As you browse through store advertisements or do your actual shopping, write down (in pencil!) the lowest price you see for each item listed in your price book, and also note which store you saw the lowest price. Whenever you're shopping and see a lower price than the one you've written in the price diary, be sure to change listings in your notebook.

Now you have a record of what the best prices are for the different items you use regularly so you can easily refer back to it. Whenever you see a sale or special offer on some item you normally purchase, you'll be able to tell at a glance if it's really a good price. This way you don't have to trust your memory about whether or not canned corn at three for a dollar is a good price for stocking up your pantry.

AVOID PREPACKAGED AND CONVENIENCE ITEMS. Not only is it usually less expensive to make your own homemade versions of convenience foods, you'll also find you have less packaging involved. This helps save the environment as well as your pocketbook. There are homemade alternatives to many regularly purchased food items such as hamburger and tuna skillet meals in a box, seasoning mixes, instant coffee beverages, cake mixes, dry soups and assorted dessert and snack items.

BEWARE OF GROCERY STORE SALES TACTICS. Often grocery stores will use creative means to lure their customers into buying more expensive items or things they wouldn't normally purchase.

A simple rule of thumb for finding bargain items on your store's shelves is this: "look high, look low." Stores often place the most expensive items at eye level. If you shop with your eyes focused on the bottom and top shelves, you're liable to find the bargains.

Many times a store will place an advertised special at the end of the aisle to catch your eye. The advertised item might be a good price, but it will often be displayed with non-sale items to try and entice you into further impulse purchases. For example, sale priced spaghetti sauce might be displayed with the store's highest priced pasta and Parmesan cheese. This is where it helps to shop from a detailed list and refer constantly to an updated price list.

Stores also offer sale items called Loss Leaders. These are the advertised specials that are so inexpensive, the store will actually take a loss by selling it at the sale price. But the purpose of these loss items is to lure more customers into the store who will then shop and buy more items that aren't on sale. If I see a great Loss Leader item at a store where I don't normally shop, I'll run in quickly if I'm in the area and only buy the sale item—nothing else. Loss Leaders are a great benefit to the customer, but you need to be aware of prices and also hold strong against impulse purchases.

USE COUPONS WISELY. Only use coupons for items and brands that you purchase normally. Many times you can find generic and store brands for a much better price than the coupon price of name brand products.

Some stores offer double coupons. If you live in those areas, this can be a great way to save quite a few extra pennies at the supermarket.

Always check the expiration date on your coupons.

Sometimes I've found coupons in my purse that I'd meant to use but forgot to give to the cashier when paying. Make a point to always hand coupons to the cashier before they start totaling your purchases. This can be done easily by matching your coupons to your shopping list and keeping them and your list in hand as you go through the store and to the checkout.

Many stores will automatically honor the store coupons of their competitors so find out if your favorite store does this. It will save you the hassle of driving around from store to store redeeming coupons. If you hate to clip coupons, look for a store that offers a bonus program where you don't need to clip coupons to get their sale prices.

Always check store flyers that come in the mail or with the newspaper for their weekly specials and private coupons. Store entrances often display special flyers. Remember to ask for a Rain Check if an advertised item isn't in stock

BUY IN BULK AND SHOP AT FOOD CO-OPS. If you have storage space, stock up on frequently used items whenever they go on sale. No room to store bulk foods or extra rolls of paper towels? Check for empty space under beds, in the attic crawl space, on the back of closet shelves or in the garage.

Be sure to check in your local area for food buying co-ops. Many have small membership fees that you'll quickly recoup from the significant savings you're able to receive on many commonly purchased items. Natural food co-ops are common and a great way to purchase organic fruits and vegetables, whole grains and other usually expensive items at competitive prices.

Some communities offer a food buying program called Share. For a minimum charge (usually about $14) and 2 hours community service, participants receive a box of food valued at $35 - $40. The community service can be something as simple as helping an elderly neighbor or working in your church nursery or Sunday School. The Share programs often offer meatless shares as well as the standard grocery items.

You can also start your own little unofficial food bulk buying co-op with a group of friends or neighbors. By purchasing items like flour, sugar, cream of wheat, oats, etc., in large bulk containers (50 pounds), you can then divide the items into family-sized amounts and split the cost.

Joining a warehouse shopping club can be a good way to save money on bulk purchases. While these stores often have lower prices than regular stores, it's still important to check per unit pricing. Sometimes you'll be surprised to find that what looked like a great deal isn't such a great deal after all. I've often found sale items at my local grocery store to be better prices per unit than the warehouse store. This is when a price book comes in handy—you won't have to rely on your memory of what constitutes a stock up price on ground meats, canned soup, etc.

Also, only buy in bulk those items that you're sure you'll be using before they go bad. Stockpiling toilet paper is a good idea since it's one of those items you know you'll be using eventually. Stockpiling bananas on sale might not be such a good idea since they spoil quickly—unless you're planning on baking with them right away or freezing banana pulp to use in recipes later.

If you do a lot of bulk buying of favorite items, you might want to consider contacting the manufacturer directly to save even more.

A freezer comes in handy for bulk purchases. I watch for sales on ground meat and when items we use frequently reach a good stock up price, I'll purchase a large amount and then repackage it into one pound bags, freezing for later use. If there are bakery outlet stores in your area, stock up on bargain priced bread, rolls, buns and dessert items, storing them in your freezer.

RESIST IMPULSE PURCHASES. It's not accidental that your local grocery store has all those handy little gadgets displayed right next to the check-out lane. How many times have we grabbed an extra snack or two as we ran through the store supposedly to just pick up a gallon of milk?

Stores count on our impulsive natures to get the better of us when we see nice displays or appetizing food items. How do we effectively battle impulse buying? In the words of a woman in Singapore, "Wait !Wait! Wait! Unless someone's dying, you don't really need that candy bar!" To contain the impulse urge, only go to the store with a specific list of needed items and stick religiously to that list.

Although this isn't related specifically to food shopping, if you're prone to impulse buying, you might want to eliminate recreational shopping as a pastime of choice. Wandering aimlessly through the mall is the perfect way to fall victim to the lure of advertising and beautiful store displays. If you really enjoy window shopping, go without your checkbook, credit cards, debit card or cash. If you see something while you're shopping that you feel you must have, if you don't have the means to buy it right then, you'll force yourself into a waiting mode. It's amazing how many times just the process of having to go back home to get the checkbook can cool the enthusiasm for that dress you couldn't live without.

Super Coupon Shopping: Real Savings?

In the book, *Miserly Moms* by Jonni McCoy, the author talks about grocery shopping using rebates and coupons, the so-called "Super Coupon

Shopping Systems." McCoy doesn't recommend a heavy reliance on coupons or rebates, and she also brings up another good point: these avid rebate fans, who can often buy $120 worth of groceries for $20, easily spend 10 - 20 hours per week on their rebate and coupon systems (reading newsletters, clipping coupons, mailing rebates, filing paperwork, etc.). Those numbers started me thinking about the amount of time that actually goes into implementing these Super Coupon programs. Was it worth investing that much of my time each week to save money on groceries?

Before I started learning about frugal grocery shopping, I easily spent $150 per week at the grocery store for a family of three. Now, with my shopping and cooking know-how, if I apply myself wholeheartedly, I can average $50 - $70 per week for a family of five.

If I were using a Super Coupon System, I would spend approximately sixty hours per month (based on the average estimate of fifteen hours per week) for about a $520 per month savings. If I were to think of my money saving activities as a part-time job, it would work out to about $8 per hour for sixty hours of work each month. (The working hours don't include time spent cooking and shopping since I'd still have to cook and shop no matter what system I was using.)

Using my own system of frugal shopping, I'd spend approximately one hour per week in menu planning, plus maybe an extra hour per week in preparing food from scratch. That equals about two hours per week—or only eight hours per month of extra work for me. Using an average amount of having spent $50 per week for groceries, I would save $400 per month on my grocery bill compared to what I used to spend. So a $400 savings from eight hours per month of work equals out to a part-time job making a whopping $50 per hour! (And who said being a stay-at-home mom doesn't pay anything?)

I don't know about you, but I'd rather work eight hours per month at $50 per hour than work 60 hours per month at $8 per hour. I have much better things to do with my time than spending my life clipping coupons and mailing in rebates. Some of that time can be used productively pursuing other avenues of life (such as writing, crafts, tutoring, etc.) that can actually open doors for additional income sources.

CHAPTER THIRTEEN
🍃 Homemade Alternatives 🍃

Throughout these past few chapters I've mentioned homemade alternatives as a tasty and viable way to save money. Here are a few of my favorite recipes that can be substituted for high-ticket items that you may usually purchase.

The following is a simple homemade alternative to those boxed hamburger or tuna skillet meals. It's also a wonderful way to use up leftovers or clean out your cupboards.

Mix-n-Match Skillet Meal
(Serves 4 to 6)

Choose ONE food from EACH of the following four groups:

BREADS AND CEREALS (1 cup raw)

Macaroni	Spaghetti
Rice (white or brown)	Noodles
Bulgar	Any pasta

SAUCE (1 can soup plus 1 ½ cans milk or water)

Cream of Potato	Cream of Chicken
Cream of Celery	Cream of Mushroom
Tomato Soup	French Onion Soup

MEAT, POULTRY, FISH OR BEANS (1 pound or ½ cup COOKED)

Chopped beef	Chopped pork or ham
Ground beef or turkey	Chicken

Turkey	Tuna
Salmon	Mackerel
Beans, cooked	Frankfurters
Keilbasa	Cooked eggs

VEGETABLES (1 ½ to 2 cups canned, cooked or raw)

Carrots	Peas
Corn	Green beans
Lima beans	Broccoli
Spinach	Mixed vegetables
Celery	Green pepper
Whatever you have around	

½ to 1 cup cheese (any kind) can be stirred into the sauce at the end of the cooking time

- Choose one food from each of the four groups above. Stir together in skillet.
- Season to taste with salt, pepper, soy sauce, onion flakes, Italian seasonings, garlic or whatever spices you enjoy.
- Bring to a boil.
- Reduce heat to lowest setting. Cover pan and simmer 30 minutes until pasta or rice is tender. Stir occasionally to prevent rice and pasta from sticking. Stir in cheese, if desired. Serve.

To bake in oven:
- Mix all ingredients in casserole dish and cover tightly.
- Bake at 350 degrees for about an hour.

I keep this Mix-n-Match Skillet Meal recipe taped to the inside of my pantry cupboard door. When I'm stuck with a "What are we having for dinner?" kind of evening, or I'm out of grocery money until the next paycheck, I can go to the cupboard and nearly always find the ingredients for some sort of skillet meal. It's a good idea to keep a record of which combinations you've tried. Some aren't really worth repeating, but others soon become family favorites.

The following is my family's all time favorite Skillet Meal combination:

International Sausage Skillet

½ to 1 pound Keilbasa (halved lengthwise and sliced thinly)

8 ounces dry pasta (I usually use penne, or medium-size tubes)

1 16-ounce can Italian-style stewed tomatoes (cut up and do NOT drain)

1 can French onion soup

In skillet, brown Keilbasa slices. Then prepare per instruction for regular Mix-n-Match Skillet Meals.

Instant Coffee Mixes

Cafe' Vienna Coffee Mix

½ cup instant coffee (regular or decaf)

1 cup powdered sugar

2/3 cup nonfat dry milk

½ teaspoon cinnamon

Use 2 heaping teaspoons per cup of hot water.

Fireside Coffee Mix

2 cups non-dairy coffee creamer

1 ½ cups hot cocoa mix

1 ½ cups instant coffee (regular or decaf)

1 ½ cups powdered sugar

1 teaspoon ground cinnamon

½ teaspoon ground nutmeg

Combine all ingredients in large bowl, stirring well. Store in airtight container. To make one cup, spoon two heaping tablespoons of mix into coffee mug. Add one cup boiling water, stir until well blended.

Cream Soup Substitute

3 tablespoons butter, margarine or oil

3 tablespoons flour

¼ teaspoon salt

dash pepper

1 ¼ cup liquid, milk or soup stock

Melt butter in saucepan. Stir in flour and seasonings. Cook over medium heat until bubbly. Add liquid slowly, stirring with wire whisk to prevent lumps from forming. Cook until thickened. Makes 1 cup condensed soup.

TOMATO: Use tomato juice for liquid. Add dash of each: garlic, onion powder, basil and oregano.

CHICKEN: Use chicken broth for half the liquid. Add ¼ teaspoon sage.

MUSHROOM or CELERY: Sauté ¼ cup chopped mushrooms or celery with 1 tablespoon minced onion in butter before adding flour.

Dry Onion Soup Mix

1 ½ cups dry minced onion

8 teaspoons onion powder

2/3 cup beef-flavored bouillon powder

½ teaspoon celery seed, crushed

½ teaspoon sugar

Mix ingredients together. Store in airtight container.

To Use: use 2 Tablespoons mix to every one cup of hot water. Simmer covered for 15 minutes.

Frozen Pop Recipes

FUDGE POPS: Prepare instant chocolate pudding according to package directions. Pour into pop molds. Freeze.

ROCKY ROAD POPS: Prepare instant chocolate pudding according to packages directions. Stir in ½ cup miniature marshmallows, ¼ cup semi-sweet chocolate chips, and ¼ cup chopped nuts (peanuts or walnuts). Pour into pop molds. Freeze.

BUTTERSCOTCH POPS: Prepare instant butterscotch pudding according to package directions, substituting root beer for milk in recipe. Pour into pop molds. Freeze.

TOFFEE POPS: Prepare instant vanilla pudding according to package directions. Stir in ½ cup chopped chocolate-covered toffee bars. Pour into pop molds. Freeze.

FRUITY POPS: Stir one cup boiling water into 1 (4-serving size) package gelatin dessert and ¼ cup sugar. Stir until dissolved. Stir in 1 ½ cups cold water. Mix in fruit (if used). Pour into pop molds. Freeze.

SIMPLE FRUITY POP VARIATIONS:
Strawberry: use strawberry gelatin with 1 cup pureed strawberries.
Lemonade: use lemon gelatin and ¼ cup lemon juice.
Watermelon: use watermelon gelatin and 1 cup pureed watermelon (seeds removed)
Orange Cream: use orange gelatin and 1 cup evaporated milk in place of water.
Use your imagination! Freezer pops made with gelatin desserts don't drip as much as pops made from drink mixes.

YOGURT POPS: Mix together 2 cups plain yogurt, 1 cup milk, 1 cup mashed fruit (your choice: strawberries, peaches, applesauce, pineapple, or 1/3 cup frozen concentrate orange or grape juice, or 6 tablespoons jam or preserves), 1 tablespoon sugar, and ½ teaspoon vanilla. Blend until smooth. Pour into pop molds. Freeze.

Ice Cream Sandwiches
In large bowl, mix together 1 package instant vanilla pudding mix and 1 ¼ cups milk. Chill briefly in refrigerator (5 minutes). Gently fold in 8-ounces frozen whipped topping. Spread pudding mixture thickly (about ½ inch) onto 10 chocolate flavored graham crackers. Top each pudding filled cracker gently with a second cracker. Place sandwiches in

a single layer on a cookie sheet. Freeze until firm (1 - 2 hours). Wrap individually with plastic wrap or foil. Store in freezer.

Breakfast Recipes

Swedish Oven Pancakes (Dutch Babies)
½ cup flour
½ cup milk
2 eggs, lightly beaten
Pinch nutmeg
4 tablespoons margarine, or butter
In bowl mix together eggs, flour, milk and nutmeg. Melt margarine. Pour margarine into a 10-inch oven proof skillet, or a 9-inch pie pan. Add batter to skillet or pie pan. Bake at 425 F for 15 to 20 minutes. Remove from oven and cut into 4 to 6 pie-shaped pieces. Serve with either maple syrup, fresh berries, fruit sauce, or lemon juice and powdered sugar. Serves 1 - 2 people. Most ovens will easily hold three pans of Dutch Babies to serve more people.

Buttermilk Pancakes
2 cups buttermilk (or substitute 2 tablespoons vinegar or lemon juice and regular milk to make 2 cups; let sit for several minutes after mixing before using)
2 cups flour
2 teaspoons baking powder
1 teaspoon baking soda
1 tsp. salt (or less)
2 eggs, lightly beaten
In bowl, mix together all ingredients in order given. Pour ¼ cup measure batter onto moderately hot oiled griddle. Turn when bubbles burst and don't fill back in quickly. Cook until browned on second side.

French Toast Casserole

This recipe provides a good way to use bread or hot dog buns that are about to go stale. Prepare this the night before so it has time to set before baking.

6 - 8 slices bread, or 1 package of 6 - 8 hot dog buns (split in half)

5 eggs

½ teaspoon vanilla

½ cup water or milk

2 tablespoons butter (or margarine)

½ cup brown sugar

In bowl, beat together eggs, vanilla and water (or milk). In a well-buttered 13x9-inch pan, place bread (or buns) in a single layer to fully cover bottom of pan. Pour egg mixture over bread. Dot with butter. Sprinkle with brown sugar. Place in refrigerator to sit overnight (can be baked right away, but better if sets for several hours). Bake at 350 F for 20 - 25 minutes.

Bean Soup Mix

(makes four packages of beans/seasonings)

2 cups dry black beans

2 cups dry Great Northern beans (or any small white bean)

2 cups dry red kidney beans

2 cups dry pinto beans

2 cups dry green split peas

In four 1-pint canning jars, layer beans in order given, dividing evenly between jars. For seasoning packets, use four individual small sandwich bags, or four 6-inch squares of plastic wrap or foil.

Into EACH seasoning packet (you'll need four times this amount total for all four jars of soup mix), place:

3 teaspoons beef or vegetable bouillon

3 tablespoons dried chives (chopped)

1 teaspoon salt

1 teaspoon dried savory

½ teaspoon ground cumin

½ teaspoon black pepper

1 bay leaf

To prepare soup:

3 hours before serving, rinse beans with cold, running water. Remove stones or shriveled beans. In a Dutch oven or stockpot, bring beans and 9 cups water to boil for 3 minutes. Remove from heat and let sit for 1 hour. Drain and rinse beans. Place beans, 5 cups of water, and seasoning packet contents into pot. Heat to boiling, reduce heat to low and simmer gently for 1 ½ hours until beans are tender. Stir occasionally. Add one 16-ounce can stewed tomatoes with liquid (break up tomatoes). Heat to boiling. Reduce to low, and cook 15 minutes more. Discard bay leaf. Each jar of soup mix will make approximately 6 - 8 generous servings.

A Simple Choice

Part Four
🍃 Simplified Housekeeping 🍃

CHAPTER FOURTEEN

🍃 Simplified Housekeeping 🍃

"...I had been well on my way to becoming so involved in taking care of things that I would have found no time to be a caretaker of people." –Karen Burton Mains, *Open Heart, Open Home*

Housework and I haven't always been friends. It's been a struggle over the past twenty years of my married life to learn the habit of keeping a neat and orderly home. Some days I'm more successful at it then others, but I'm learning and growing in this area constantly.

I've often found that reading assorted books by housework "experts" are more depressing than they are inspiring for those of us who are a bit domestically challenged. Yes, these experts know what they're doing. But so often I don't feel like they have even a glimpse of how difficult basic housekeeping can be for someone who just doesn't seem to have it in their genes to do it naturally.

Probably the biggest motivator for me to find a way to keep my house neat was realizing very early in my marriage that I now had some-one else living in the house with me. I wasn't a teenager anymore with a messy bedroom that didn't affect anyone but me. Now someone else needed to function amidst the chaos and clutter that naturally found it's way into my living spaces. Neatness and order were important to my new husband. Since I cared about his comfort and happiness, it became important to me to help keep the house in a semi-respectable state of orderliness so he could enjoy his home and his new marriage. Please don't think my husband never lifted a finger around the house to clean (he's always been great about those things), but since our early married years were spent with him working full-time and me attending college, I felt I had a bit more time to devote to the basic maintenance of our home (although full-time college probably counts as a full-time job, too—but I digress).

Over the years, I've learned a few tricks that have helped me tremendously. Just so you know, I'm still a work-in-progress in the area of housekeeping. But because of my desire to simplify my life and keep things from getting too complicated, I'm hoping some of the tricks I've learned will prove helpful to others as well.

Ten Minute Tidy

One of the most helpful and simplest things my children and I do to maintain our home is something we've dubbed the Ten Minute Tidy. What it involves is this: everyone runs around the house picking up clutter and putting it away as fast they can for ten minutes.

Whenever I notice that the main living areas of the house are getting that well lived-in look, I call for a Ten Minute Tidy. Everyone drops whatever they're doing and then flies into "pick-up-the-stuff" mode. I actually set a kitchen timer for ten minutes and when it goes off, we're done. Usually I tidy the kitchen and main bathroom myself, while the kids tidy the living room, family room and, if there's still time left, their bedrooms. It's amazing how quickly the house can go from looking messy to looking neat when everyone works fast, works together and works smart.

The purpose of the Ten Minute Tidy isn't to actually deep clean the house, but to tidy up the rooms so our home looks neat and livable again. The cleaning and regular maintenance is done during a scheduled "Upkeep" time each day. I always focus the Ten Minute Tidy on the areas that make a first impression when people enter my home. In our case, that's the entry/hallway, living room, kitchen/family area and main bath.

"Times-Up" Upkeep

The Time's Up Upkeep is the way I've started doing the daily maintenance of our housekeeping tasks. This concept also requires the use of the kitchen timer—although for this idea you won't be moving as quickly as with the Ten Minute Tidy.

To do a Time's Up Upkeep, I first mentally divided my home into six areas: 1) kitchen/dining area, 2) living/family rooms, 3) bathrooms (I count both bathrooms as one area), 4) laundry room, 5) master bedroom, 6) kids' bedrooms.

The children are responsible for their own rooms in this cleaning strategy so I only count their rooms as one area. I act as Supervisor for all three kids' rooms, although the youngest needs a lot more help than just simple supervising at this point in her life. As she learns more and is trained in proper clean up procedures, I'll move from the teaching mode to the supervising mode with her as well.

The procedure for a Time's Up Upkeep is this: spend thirty minutes (just five minutes in each area of the house) straightening, cleaning and putting away. Start with the biggest and most obvious things in the room: the bed in a bedroom, the table and counters in the kitchen, the sink and counters in the bathroom, etc. When the five minute time frame is over in one room, move to the next—don't keep working in the first room, or you may find yourself bogged down and never moving on to the other areas of your home. Just be sure to finish whatever you're currently working on (don't leave the bed unmade). The rest of the clean up will be waiting for you tomorrow.

It's amazing the difference you'll start to see after just a couple days of doing a Time's Up Upkeep. Since you obviously won't need to dust each room everyday and when you've finished some of the basic maintenance in each room, you'll be able to move onto activities like cleaning out drawers or closets. It may be just one drawer a day, but after a week of cleaning out drawers, you may find yourself actually astonished at the difference in your home.

If you have an area of your house that desperately needs to be cleaned out and sorted through, but you find that you're overwhelmed by even starting the task (garage, attic, hall closet), add an extra five minutes to your daily Time's Up Upkeep and start working on that scary project one little step at a time. Do you remember the instructions on how to eat an elephant? Just take one bite at a time. The same principle applies with those monumental projects that we keep putting off until another day. Just five to ten minutes a day and before you know it, you'll find yourself at the end of a completed project.

I try to set the goal of having our Time's Up Upkeep in the morning before we leave the house for any outside activities, but on some days, that's not a realistic goal. I've found that coming home to a neat and orderly house is such a wonderful feeling, so I try not to leave the house without at least a quick Ten Minute Tidy.

Before I go to bed at night, I do a quick run through of the living areas of the house. I pick up newspapers, put dishes in the dishwasher, clear off tables and countertops and just do a very brief tidy time. It makes a world of difference to get up in the morning and face a picked up house, rather than being greeted by yesterday's messes first thing in the morning.

Pink Bunnies

While talking to my daughter recently, we discussed the need for decluttering her bedroom. Over the years, she's collected quite an array of toys, books, decorative objects and miscellaneous odds and ends. She tends to bond emotionally to anything that enters her room, so getting her to willingly clear out the excess "stuff" has usually been quite an ordeal.

I've learned over the years that the more clutter and excess stuff I carry with me, the more disorganized and scattered my life feels. My daughter and I looked around her room and I asked her, "When you look at the piles of papers and toys in your room, do you feel overwhelmed by it all—not even sure where to start when you need to clean your room?"

She agreed that was just how she felt. Many of the items I saw in her room were things she never used or played with anymore. But she also had special items that held significant meaning to her.

I suddenly had an idea.

I grabbed her all-time favorite toys (the ones that were "real" in the Velveteen Rabbit sense of the word), and held them up to her. "Big Bird and Fluffy are special toys, right? They're your comforting friends, your buddies you sleep with each night. They've seen you through surgeries and scary times. You'll probably want to keep them forever." She smiled and nodded as she realized I knew how much her favorite stuffed animals meant to her.

Then I grabbed two pink bunnies from under her bed that she never played with, they were nothing special to her, just plain old pink bunnies. "Now look at these pink bunnies. Do you want to lug them around with you for the rest of your life? They're nice bunnies. They're even cute bunnies. But are they special bunnies?"

She laughed at the idea of lugging the pink bunnies around forever, and agreed they weren't anything she played with or thought much about.

As we looked around and discussed her toys, she realized her room was full of other "Pink Bunnies"—those items that just took up space, cluttering up her closet, dresser and floor. I suggested she make two piles of things in her room: the "Pink Bunny" pile and the "Big Bird and Fluffy" pile. If something wasn't a favorite item that she used regularly, it belonged in the "Pink Bunny" pile. Items that brought her joy, had particular meaning, and were used frequently would be put in the "Big Bird and Fluffy" pile.

Suddenly it became not only easy to sort her toys, but also fun! I'd hold up a toy and ask, "What's this one?"

She'd laugh and say, "It's a Pink Bunny!" and then happily toss it into the pile of toys destined for the garage sale bin. The Pink Bunnies seemed to outnumber the special toys by about three to one. After she sorted through the toys, she found that she had a nice manageable pile of her very favorite toys. Not only did it reduce the clutter in her room, but it also brought her a great sense of accomplishment. She finally was able to sort through everything and part with the things she didn't use anymore.

How many Pink Bunnies do you have in your house and your life? Maybe it's time to sort through the clutter and find out.

Toys

I've heard from many people that one of the biggest clutter problems in their home is their children's toys. After realizing you've let your children accumulate too many toys, what's a parent to do?

One easy step to prevent a further build up of toys is to make a rule that for every new toy that comes into the house, an old toy goes out. If there's a large build up of already established toys, you might want to make the rule that for every new toy that enters the home, two (or even three!) old toys go out.

I've also found that by appealing to my children's altruistic tendencies, I've had success convincing them to part with toys they don't play with anymore. I've encouraged my children to donate their gently used toys to organizations that will distribute these toys to other children who might not otherwise have any toys at all. Now that my children are a bit older, they're also motivated to part with toys if they know they can sell the items at our next family garage sale and keep the money themselves (not quite as altruistic a motive, but effective for decluttering their rooms nonetheless).

The Kitchen

Probably the best way to keep from accumulating clutter is by not allowing it into your house to begin with. Don't buy extra stuff in the first place. I've found that kitchen clutter can get out of hand almost as quickly as children's toys. Recently I dug through my drawers and cabinets trying to identify only the items I used regularly. It was amazing how many single-purpose items I found hiding in my kitchen. I'd personally rather have one utensil that can be used for any number of purposes (such as a sharp, good quality chef's knife—it dices, it slices, it minces, it chops, etc.), than a collection of five or six single purpose doodads cluttering up my precious cabinet space and drawers.

Quick Housekeeping Tips

- When cleaning your house, start with any "dry" jobs first (vacuuming, sweeping, dusting, etc.) before you start with the "wet" clean-up (mopping, spray cleansers, sponging, etc.).

- Clean everything from top to bottom since dirt and water run downhill.

- Save yourself some scrubbing by first wetting the things you're cleaning with cleansers and then allowing the cleaning solution to sit for awhile. Dried on gunk on the countertop will be a breeze to wipe off after it's been sitting in cleaning solution for five to ten minutes.

- Use crumpled newsprint to clean windows. It won't streak, smudge or leave lint on your windows.

- Always vacuum before you dust since the vacuum will stir up dust in the air, depositing it back onto your furniture.

- Buy versatile cleaning products that do more than one cleaning task. This will save you both time and money.

- To prevent dust build up from static on television screens and computer monitors, use a pre-used fabric softener sheet for dusting rather than a normal dusting cloth.

- To remove water spots from fine wood furniture, use an old toothbrush and baking soda. Wrap the toothbrush bristles in a soft, slightly damp cloth and dip into baking soda. Rub gently to remove water spot.

- To remove crayon marks from walls or permanent ink marks from countertops, use a dampened stiff wool cloth and gently rub in one direction repeatedly. Don't scrub.

- To hide nail holes in white painted walls, fill the holes with a dab of plain white toothpaste (no green specks or gels). Wipe off excess. If you're going to repaint the walls, allow the toothpaste to dry for at least 24 hours before painting.

- Keep a row of pegs or hooks just inside your front door. Have children hang their school backpacks on the pegs as soon as they walk through the door each afternoon.

- To clean the surface of a vinyl doll, sprinkle lightly with baking soda and gently rub with a slightly damp cloth. Wipe and dry each part of the doll as you finish a section so the baking soda doesn't dry on the surface.

- To quickly clean the surface of stuffed animal toys that can't be washed in water, rub cornstarch into the fur and then vacuum with the brush attachment.

- For a stale smelling room, sprinkle a combination of baking soda and a small amount of spice (cinnamon, nutmeg or cloves) onto the carpet. Let it sit for awhile and then vacuum as usual.

- Put a small amount of favorite potpourri directly into the vacuum cleaner bag. Every time you vacuum the carpet, the scent will be released throughout the house.

- For a quick scent pick-me-up for the house place a small saucepan filled with hot water onto the stovetop to simmer. Add a combination of cinnamon, cloves, vanilla and orange peels (if available). After simmering for a few minutes, the house will smell good enough to eat!

Bathroom Tips

- To prevent mold and mildew growth, be sure to adequately ventilate the bathroom, using exhaust fans and opening windows after a bath or shower.

- To keep mirrors from fogging while taking a shower, drape the mirror with a towel before you start showering.

- To defog mirrors quickly and easily, point your blow dryer at it for a few seconds. The hot air will quickly evaporate the moisture on the mirror.

- To keep mirrors from fogging, polish with a thin coating of liquid soap using a dry paper towel or wadded newspaper (no water!). This will keep your mirrors relatively fog-free for several weeks.

- Every six months, take your shower head apart and soak the pieces over night in white vinegar. This removes any build up and makes your showering more efficient.

- To prevent dog hair from clogging your bathtub drain while giving Fido his bath, place a piece of steel wool over the drain in place of the regular hair catcher.

- To remove food odors, keep a few charcoal briquettes on a small plate in the refrigerator.

- To organize each person's toiletries in the bathroom cupboard, give everyone their own covered shoe box for storing brushes, make-up, personal cleansers, etc.

- Store cotton balls in an empty tissue box. Looks much nicer than the big plastic bags cotton balls usually come in.

- For the sake of guests, always keep an extra roll of toilet paper in plain sight.

- Periodically clean your hair brushes and combs. Run a comb through the hairbrush to remove hair, then soak combs and brushes for 20 minutes in a sudsy mixture of warm water and liquid dish detergent or shampoo. Rinse thoroughly with warm water.

- Store soap slivers in a clean heavy-duty glass jar. When it's full, pour boiling water over slivers. Stir. Use as liquid soap when cool.

- Train your family to always close the lid of the toilet before flushing. The flushing action forms an aerosol spray containing whatever is in the toilet and then sends the germ-laden mist throughout the room.

Bedroom and Closet Tips

- A bed covered with a comforter rather than a bedspread is easier to make, especially for children.

- To clean dusty throw pillows or soft fabric dolls, just toss into the dryer on the "Air Fluff" (no heat) setting for about ten minutes.

- Clean the surface of vinyl water bed mattresses once a month. Sponge the top and sides with a mild solution of dishwashing liquid. Rinse thoroughly with clear water. Dry.

- When not in use, put large luggage pieces to work storing off-season clothing or hiding holiday gifts.

- Closets can sometimes become stale and smelly if they're not ventilated properly. Once a month, leave the closet doors open overnight. To remove odors, sprinkle a layer of baking soda on the floor and leave for several hours. Then vacuum thoroughly. You can also tape a wrapper from a scented bar of soap to the back wall behind the clothes to freshen the closet.

- Can't stand the smell of mothballs? Use small cloth bags to hold whole cloves. Hang the clove-filled bags in closets and place in pockets of clothes.

- Keep an open basket on the top shelf of your coat closet for storing winter items like scarves, mittens, etc. When you find a long lost mitten at the back of your four-year-old's closet in mid-summer, simply throw it into the basket and it'll be right where you need it when the cold weather comes.

Garage Tips

- Use plain clay kitty litter to absorb oil leaks on the floor.

- Hang frequently used tools on a pegboard with "S" hooks. You can even outline the tools so you always know what goes where (and can easily identify what's missing).

- Use baking soda to polish chrome on your car.

- To reduce odor, whenever you change the cat's litter box sprinkle ½ cup baking soda into the kitty litter.

- To cover small scratches on your car's surface and prevent rust damage, choose a child's crayon in a matching color. Rub it gently into the scratch and it will give a coating of wax. Wipe off excess.

Kitchen Tips

- Prevent many spill-overs on the stove by using bigger pots and pans. Most cooking-related spills come from using too small of a pot.

- To remove dried or cooked on food spills from the stovetop, bring some water to a rolling boil and then carefully pour some boiling water onto the dried spill. Allow to sit for several minutes, then wipe off. Repeat if necessary.

- To sweeten the smell of your garbage disposal, toss in a few citrus rinds (lemon, grapefruit, orange or lime) from time to time.

- To remove coffee or tea stains from fine china, put ½ teaspoon baking soda and hot water into each stained tea cup. Let soak overnight. Scrub lightly with soft cloth; rinse.

- To prevent splatters when frying meat on the stove, add a dash of salt to the oil before heating.

- Use your dishwasher for cleaning more than plates and flatware. Use it to wash: stove burner liners, grills from outdoor barbecues, metal filters above the stove, children's plastic toys on the top rack (for example, hard plastic blocks placed in mesh bags), glass knick-knacks, candleholders.

- If you use cloth napkins, get a different shaped napkin holder for each member of the family. Everyone can use their same napkin all day long, and then replace the dirty napkins with fresh ones for using the next day.

- To absorb stale odors, wipe down floors, countertops, cabinets, with a mixture of half water / half white vinegar. After the vinegar smell dissipates, things will smell much fresher. You can also use a small pan filled with vinegar to keep on hand as an on-going air freshener. This works especially well with kitchen odors and smoke.

Laundry Tips

- Use one cup white vinegar in the rinse cycle as a fabric softener. It also freshens the clothes' smell.

- To wash delicate articles of clothing in your washing machine, place them in a pillowcase and tie it shut. Launder on gentle cycle as usual.

- To remove wrinkles from machine dried clothing, try putting a slightly damp towel into the dryer after the clothes are already dry, then turn on the dryer again for five minutes.

- It's better to gently retreat a spot two or three times, rather than scrubbing vigorously only once.

- Baby socks tend to get lost in the wash. Either place all tiny baby items in a zippered mesh bag to wash, or use a safety pin to attach baby socks to a larger item in the wash.

- To remove blood stains from white fabrics, use a dab or two of hydrogen peroxide.

CHAPTER FIFTEEN
🍃 Pilers and Filers 🍃

"The ordinary arts we practice every day at home are of more importance to the soul than their simplicity might suggest." –Thomas Moore

I have a friend, Karen Jogerst, who teaches classes on household management and has written a book called, *If I Could Just Get Organized! Home Management Hope for Pilers and Filers* (ordering information in the resource section). Karen has a slightly different twist on organizational techniques, and her ideas and methods have helped me more than anything else I've read on this topic.

Karen teaches that there are basically two types of personal organization styles: Filers and Pilers. Filers are those highly organized, "a-place-for-everything-and-everything-in-it's-place" type of housekeepers. They're the ones with the neat and tidy underwear drawers, their closets are color-coded, and their canned goods are alphabetized.

And Pilers are . . . well . . . they're Pilers. (I'm often a Piler Extraordinaire.)

Karen teaches that Messies are simply Pilers who are attempting to be Filers. She says that if you try to organize things contrary to your personal organizational nature, you're dooming yourself to failure. Pilers who try to be Filers often get frustrated, give up and then let the piles overrun their homes—thus becoming Messies.

An Organized Piler

I asked Karen one day, "So tell me, how on earth do Pilers organize their things? I can't live with all this clutter anymore. Mount Fold-Me in the laundry room is about to suffer a major landslide and the paper piles are overrunning every room. Help!"

She told me the secret to successful organization for Pilers is to contain the piles, and to keep up on sorting through your piles, looking for throw away trash on a regular basis. She's a Piler herself, so she understands firsthand how difficult this can be.

Karen gave an example of a Piler's kitchen cupboards. The cupboards usually just have things thrown in helter-skelter, falling out every time the door is opened. Rather than trying to organize the madness, a Piler needs to contain the piles. If there are bags of dry beans falling over each other, get a small cardboard box that fits into the cupboard, cut a scoop out of the front of it and toss dry beans into that container. The beans are still piled, but the pile is now neatly contained. Do the same for seasoning packets, baby food or whatever else is causing havoc in your cupboards. You'll end up with a cupboard full of neatly contained piles.

If you find a place in your house that collects piles at an alarming rate, you'll need to identify what you've piled there and then make containers for the various piles.

The Piles of My Life

My worst "Piler" nightmare for years was the pile of stuff on top of the dryer in my laundry room. Not only was it probably a fire hazard, it drove me nuts. At the time that I finally conquered Mount Fold-Me, I had a tiny laundry room with virtually no floor space or counters. It wasn't a separate room, either. It was right off my kitchen where we all had to look at it while eating. Not a pretty or appetizing sight, believe me.

When standing in that cramped little corner doing laundry, I had been pulling clean and dry clothes out of the dryer, folding them immediately and then piling everything into a single laundry basket balanced on the top edge of the dryer's control panel—intending to move the neatly folded clothes to their proper drawers and closets before I did another load of laundry. It didn't take long for the pile to overflow onto the dryer. The pile would often get so high, I couldn't see the top of it—and neither could my six-foot-two husband.

Someone in the family was always asking, "Do I have any clean socks?"

"Yes," I'd say. "They're in the pile on the dryer."

The poor person who just wanted a clean pair of socks would have to go digging through that precarious mountain of clothes. Invariably, some small unsuspecting child would end up with a pile of clothes on top of them.

"Mom! Help me!"

Needless to say, this wasn't an efficient approach to laundry, but this poor Piler was clueless about what to do differently.

Identifying the Piles

Enter the idea about containing the piles. I stood in my laundry room one day for about an hour, analyzing what was in that ominous, leaning pile on top of my dryer:
- clothes for five people
- clean, folded clothes
- clean, unfolded clothes
- a myriad of unmatched, clean socks
- a few odds and ends of school supplies
- clothes my kids had outgrown (and needed to be taken to the garage for the charity bag)

"Okay," I thought, "According to Karen, I need to contain the piles. But how?"

I didn't have any extra floor space in the room. Then I noticed a one and a half foot wide spot behind the back door. Another ominous pile of things was beginning to accumulate there: paint cans, recycling bags and boxes of outgrown clothes to name a few. Obviously I'd just found more things that needed to be contained.

Suddenly I realized that all the stuff behind the door was being piled in a small bit of floor space. I wondered if shelves would fit there? I measured. Sure enough, there was just enough room for a steel shelving unit I'd seen at the store.

Hmmmm . . . .

Now, how many containers would I need? I figured it out. I would need: one for my clothes, one for my husband's clothes, one for each of three children, one for unmatched socks, one for recycling, one for odds and ends of school supplies and one for outgrown clothes. Nine pile containers all together.

Containing the Piles

So I headed off to the store to look at potential pile containers. I wanted something eye-pleasing since this shelf of pile containers would be within constant view of my kitchen and dining area. I found some narrow wicker laundry baskets and carried them over to the shelving unit I had in mind. They fit perfectly—two baskets per shelf.

I came home, set up the shelving which just fit behind the back door, labeled the baskets with little tags (Mommy's, Daddy's, socks, etc.), and then proceeded to sort through the pile on the dryer: Daddy's shirt goes there, son's underwear goes there, baby's dress goes there, box of colored pencils goes there. I found I could just toss them into their appropriate containers since the shelving was right next to the washer/dryer. Absolutely brainless and painless laundry sorting.

Later in the day, my son came up to me with the usual lament, "Mommy, I don't have any clean socks."

With a sense of satisfaction I said, "They're in the sock basket, honey."

And you know what? Amazingly enough, they were! My son still needed to sort through and find a matching pair, but it just took a second or two, rather than the long process it was before the socks were contained in their own separate pile.

Now when I have an extra few minutes, or when the kids are bored (heaven forbid!), we can grab the sock basket and start sorting. After the socks are sorted and folded, we can just throw the socks into the appropriate pile containers on the shelf.

When it's time to put away laundry, I just have everyone come and pick up their respective laundry baskets, each family member takes their clothes to their rooms, puts their clothes away and then brings back their basket to the shelf.

You can hardly imagine how neat my laundry room looked after containing the piles. Also, because I was now working within the realm of my natural Piler tendencies, this was a solution that would work for the long haul.

Can you all say, "Hooray?"

Next step for me: containing the piles in my kitchen cupboards.

Try this method if you find you are suffering from piles in your own home. Whatever room it is that stresses you the most, begin there. Once you realize the efficiency of this method for yourself, you'll be inspired to move to other rooms in the home.

CHAPTER SIXTEEN
🍂 Kids and Clean-Up 🍂

"There should be less talk; a preaching point is not a meeting point. What do you do then? Take a broom and clean someone's house. That says enough."—Mother Teresa

I know what some of you are thinking, "How in the world do the words 'kids' and 'cleaning' go together?" Well, I'm no expert on the topic personally, but I went to someone who has successful experience in this area and asked her advice.

Several years ago, my friend Lisa, wife and mother of three, developed a difficult and chronic illness that left her unable to do much more than move from her bed, to the couch, to the bathroom and back to bed. It was several weeks before I was able to stop by to visit her after she first became ill. Knowing how badly my house would fall apart if I was laid up for weeks on end, I was expecting to find a home that was cluttered and messy. I was going to offer to clean up for her while I visited.

I expected to see piles of unwashed dishes, baskets full of unwashed laundry, dirty floors and newspapers all over. What I saw almost took my breath away. Her home looked as neat and nice as it always had. I knew that they hadn't hired a maid, so I was left wondering how this apparent housekeeping magic had occurred.

Then I noticed something. Her three children (two were teenagers at this point) were in the room. One went over and started to empty the dishwasher without being asked. It suddenly dawned on me that her house had stayed so nice because her children had been well trained to help around the house. The entire job of housekeeping was a family affair, not just the domain of one person.

Since my children were small at this time, I recognized that a great deal more of the household responsibilities were going to fall on the shoulders of the adults in the home, but during that visit to Lisa's house, I caught a glimpse of how I wanted my home to run when my kids were older. I knew that in order to see that happen, it was going to require work on my part to help my children learn to do the various jobs correctly, and then help them to learn good housekeeping habits.

Lisa's house didn't fall apart when her health suffered because her children were in the habit of keeping up on their daily chores. Their family also didn't have a lot of arguments or disagreements about chores, since it wasn't something up for debate. It was simply a habit instilled in the children from the time they were young. Not only do I believe that this habit will help her children later in life when they have homes of their own, but I believe it's also a way to instill good work habits that will carry over into other areas of their lives as well. As children grow to adults, they'll be better workers when they enter the work force, making them a valuable asset to their employers.

I finally called Lisa one day and asked her to give me the details of what they had done with their children to reach this level of teamwork and good housekeeping habits. I wanted to be able to apply the same techniques in my home with my three children. Here are some of her tips.

Job Descriptions

One of the most important aspects of their household clean up and daily maintenance has been developing job titles for certain groups of chores. The job titles come complete with full job descriptions. Each child is given a particular job and then the jobs are rotated each week. A younger child will work more closely with a parent to accomplish these duties, but an older child or teen will often be able to handle the jobs completely by themselves.

Here are a couple examples of possible job titles and descriptions—these are probably the three most basic job titles that you want to make sure are assigned to someone each week. Create the same number of jobs as you have children so everyone has an assignment.

ASSISTANT COOK: Helps at each meal every day, helps the parent cook and prepare meals, learns to cook, does whatever they're capable of handling on their own, sets the table.

CLEAN UP CREW: Hand washes whatever needs to be hand washed (pots, pans, china), loads and runs the dishwasher, washes tables, cleans off stove and countertops, sweeps kitchen, sweeps or vacuums dining room floor.

RECYCLER/GARBAGE COLLECTOR: Empties all small garbage cans and waste baskets, cleans around cans, separates recycling (tin cans, aluminum, empty milk jugs, newspapers, laundry cartons, cardboard).

Depending on the number of children you have to work with in your family, you can be creative and make as many job titles and descriptions as you need. Other possibilities: Bathroom Duty (tub, tile, sink, mirrors, floor, toilet, towels, etc.), Laundry (collect, sort, wash, dry, fold, put away, tidy laundry room), General Maid (vacuuming, dusting, windows, mirrors). You can even assign specific job titles to adults living in the house, too.

I saw this job description idea in action one year when we invited Lisa and her family to have Thanksgiving dinner with us. During the preparation time for dinner, I found that their youngest son was constantly at my elbow asking what he could do to help. It was wonderful to have such a willing and able helper. His job that week for the family was kitchen duty and since the children's jobs apply to every meal every day, he was even helping me at my house by doing his expected job.

Then when the meal was over, their daughter popped out of her seat and immediately started helping with clearing the table and doing the dishes. Her job that week was Clean Up Crew, so there she was helping me cheerfully—just like she would've been doing at home.

After seeing their kids in action at my house helping out with the holiday meal, I knew for sure that this was an idea I wanted to put into practice in my own home.

Chore Charts

The basic job descriptions listed above will help get a great deal of the work around the house completed in a timely and simple way, but there are still chores that fall out of the range of the job descriptions. What do we do with those?

This is where a weekly Chore Chart can come in handy. All those loose ends that still need to be tied up can find their way onto a chart on the refrigerator. Lisa told me that they simply have a sheet of paper with 18 boxes on it—three rows down for each of the three children and six rows across for each day of the week (minus Sunday). At the beginning of each week, Lisa simply divides the regular weekly chores equally between the three kids, writing the daily chores into each box. As the kids complete their assigned chores, they just check them off.

The types of chores that Lisa usually includes on the Chore Chart are any duties that don't show up in one of the Job Descriptions. In their case, chores such as laundry, vacuuming various rooms, cleaning the bathroom, dusting the living room, dusting the bedrooms and cleaning mirrors and windows show up on the Chore Chart.

Check Mark System

The Check Mark System is an additional method that not only works for helping to get some of the more difficult and less desirable jobs completed around the house but also combines a form of discipline to help with improving the children's behavior in pre-selected areas.

First, the kids come up with a list of all the awful jobs around the house that nobody wants to do (i.e.: washing the cat's litter box, pulling weeds, cleaning gutters, mowing the lawn, washing the inside and outside of the cars, cleaning glass sliding doors, washing out trash cans, sweeping the patio, scrubbing under the kitchen sink around the garbage can, cleaning the refrigerator, etc.). It's important that the kids come up with this list of awful jobs themselves. Mom and Dad can always offer suggestions, but these need to be the chores the kids don't like to do.

Write each awful chore on a small piece of paper and then put it into a container.

Next, hold a family meeting to discuss areas of behavior or attitudes that are frustrating to Mom and Dad. Only focus on two or three at a time. These areas of behavior improvement then become the list of Check Mark Rules. Some possible examples: fighting, interrupting, back talk, swearing, etc. Each family will have their own list of pet-peeves that they need to work on.

When the kids break one of the Check Mark Rules, they have a check mark put on a card next to their name. This card can just be a small index card taped to the refrigerator or post it on a family message center or bulletin board. At the end of the week, the kids get to draw the same number of awful chores that they have check marks after their name. These are then additional chores that they need to complete as soon as possible (often on Saturday).

If a particular job doesn't get drawn from the hat for awhile, the reality is that the job still needs to be done eventually. At that point, the Check Mark Chores can become jobs the kids can be paid for doing. Some weeks all the chores will be drawn due to a difficult time with improving behavior. Other weeks, the Check Mark Chores will be left undone due to improved behavior.

As the kids develop control over their current list of Check Mark Rules, you can call another family meeting and establish new Check Mark criteria. This way you can continually work on instilling good habits and eliminating those annoying little irritations from your family—while seeing that the basic upkeep around your home is accomplished in a timely fashion.

CHAPTER SEVENTEEN

🍂 Garage Sales 🍂

"Foraging gives us the ability to view the old and abandoned in a new light—reclaiming them from oblivion with creativity and choice . . ."
–Sarah Ban Breathnach, *Simple Abundance*

Now that we've sorted through our accumulation of clutter, what do we do with all the items that need to find a new place to live? For some people the best answer is to have a garage sale!

For many years, the idea of holding a Garage Sale or Yard Sale was about as appealing to me as the thought of going to the dentist for a root canal. It wasn't something I would willingly and purposefully plan into my life. When I had things that needed to be cleared out of our house, I simply set a bag on the doorstep for the latest charity that called who was having a truck in my neighborhood.

Recently I've come to recognize that holding a well-run Garage Sale can actually be a fairly profitable use of my time and effort. It's not something I would ever want to do more than once or twice a year, but now that I've discovered some tricks to the process, I've actually found it can be a fun way to spend a few days.

Recently I held a four day Garage Sale that was successful beyond my wildest dreams. Since many people often consider holding a sale of some sort rather than just carting everything off to charity, I thought I'd share some of the ideas I used during my sale for anyone who is thinking about holding a sale to clear out their gently used (or even roughly used) clutter.

Number of Days

To begin with, plan on having the sale for more than the typical one or two days. At my last sale, I decided on four days—Wednesday through Saturday. Many shoppers stopped by the first two days just out of the novelty of seeing a garage sale being held on a day different from the usual Friday/Saturday. Also, holding a sale on an off day when there aren't other sales being held around town is beneficial since customers aren't holding onto their pennies, waiting to see if there's something better at the next sale. If you're the only game in town that day, they buy!

Classified Ads

For a garage sale of more than two days in length, I placed two separate ads in the local paper. For my sale, the first ad covered Wednesday and Thursday, and the second ad was for Friday and Saturday. If you have just one advertisement that runs for all four days and says the sale goes from Wednesday to Saturday, few people will show up on the last two days of the sale. They'll think all the good stuff has already been picked over.

Be sure to double-check your ad when it appears in the newspaper. One of the days my ad ran, the newspaper misprinted some of my information. So I called the paper about it and they refunded my money.

Also, the longer your ad, the better. Most ads are fairly short, but the more substantial ads stand out better amidst long listings of garage sales. Try to list items at your sale individually: furniture, clothing, small appliances, toys, baby items, blankets, collectibles, etc. If there's anything special about your sale, mention it. I put in my ad that my sale contained five generations of junk (well, I actually wrote "treasures" in the ad itself, not "junk"). Since people always ask me this question, the five generations consisted of: #1-my kids, #2-me and hubby, #3-my parents and in-laws, #4-my grandparents, and #5-items handed down from two great-grandmothers.

Stuff

I collected bags and boxes full of all sorts of odds and ends from family and friends. I told them I was going to be holding a big garage sale, and if they had anything they were needing to clear out, I'd be happy to come by and pick it up and get rid of it for them at my sale. Everyone I approached was more than happy to contribute a bag or two.

When deciding which items to put out for sale, don't sort things according to what you think will sell and what you think won't. Try to sell everything! What's junk to one person is often someone else's treasure. Even broken appliances, lawn mowers and vacuum cleaners can be sold for parts. Also, don't throw out your old magazines. Stick them all in a box and sell them for a quarter a piece. Many parents look for old magazines to use for crafts with their children.

You'll be amazed at the things that sell. The hot items at my sale were extremely tacky costume jewelry, children's clothing, gift items and ancient sheet music from the 20's and 30's (people were buying the sheet music to frame for decorations—at my suggestion—and then a collector came along and offered to buy all the remaining sheet music for a sizable amount!).

Arrangement of Sale

Think "store" and "shopping" when you're setting up your sale. Try to imagine the traffic patterns of customers that will browse your sale. You want people to feel comfortable as they browse and shop. You don't want them just running in, glancing at piles of junk strewn haphazardly around and then running right back out the door without really looking at what you have for sale.

Before my sale, I emptied out the garage, swept it clean, and then set up three long tables in rows running from the front to the back of the garage. Since I had so much junk (I mean "treasures"), I also had two long rows of tables out in the driveway, plus multiple boxes filled with odds and ends (i.e.: "Everything in this Box - 25 cents"). I borrowed folding tables from family and friends, made makeshift tables from plywood placed over large cardboard boxes and then I covered all the tables with light colored sheets (preferably plain with no patterns so the sheets don't detract from the items on top of them). The sheet-strewn tables looked nice and also helped to show off the items displayed. Next, I made sure the garage area was well lit.

Arrange your tables according to categories: all kitchen gadgets on one table, bedding on another, clothes on another, gift items grouped together, jewelry displayed next to a mirror, etc. Decide in advance which categories of stuff you have and then sort your items. It's so much easier for people to find things they want if they can look at a table and think, "Ah . . . kitchen stuff," or "Oh, how nice . . . a table of gift items!"

Clothing

Be sure to display your clothing nicely. If you have a freestanding clothes rack, put it in the garage during your sale to hold nicer items. Clothing on a table should be sorted according to general sizes (baby things, kids' clothes, adult men, adult women), and folded and stacked neatly. I had to go back over to the clothing table several times each day and re-stack, re-fold and re-sort the clothes, but it was worth the effort. Almost everything sold—even stained clothing and jeans with holes in the knees. People don't like digging through piles and piles of mix-and-matched junk clothing, but when they see everything looking nice and neat—displayed like they'd see it in a store—they quite happily stand there and sort through the items.

I also washed all clothing and stuffed animals before putting them out for the sale. It not only made the items more attractive, but you can get a higher price for these items if they look as close to "new" as possible.

Rather than pricing each piece of clothing individually, I just put a big easy-to-read sign over the table. I hung my sign on cardboard from the garage rafters at eye-level right over the clothing table. I sold clothes for "50 cents each or three for $1—unless otherwise marked."

Soft Background Music

One of the most important tips (you're probably going to think it's crazy—but trust me) is playing quiet background music while people shop. Set a mood conducive to shopping. Don't play music that's loud or too lively as people will be apt to shop quickly. You want people to relax . . . shop . . . take their time . . . enjoy the process. An easy-listening station that plays familiar songs from the 70's and 80's would be ideal. People will hum and sing as they shop—maybe not leave until their favorite song is over.

I personally chose a Classical music station (the normal station I listen to) since I had to sit there all day for four days listening to the music, too—I didn't want to lose my mind listening to music I don't normally play (although I'm sure a lot of people would lose their mind listening to Classical all day!). Customers enjoyed the music though, and several even commented about what a nice tone it set to my Garage Sale.

One morning, I was noticing that people weren't browsing like they had been; they were just running in, looking quickly, and then running out again and not buying anything. This seemed strange since that hadn't been the tone of the sale previously. Suddenly it dawned on me that I'd forgotten to turn on the radio. Within just a few minutes of playing quiet background music again, the shoppers slowed down, took their time and started buying things, again. That quiet, soothing music completely changed everything.

Odds-and-Ends Tips

- On those large colorful signs that you post around town for your sale, be sure to list some of the items at your sale: tools, baby items, clothing, housewares, collectibles, etc.
- Stock up on bags from the grocery store so you can offer to bag up purchases for those customers with armloads of small items.
- Make people comfortable. Since I've worked for many years in "people" oriented jobs, this practically comes as second nature to me, but I've been to so many garage sales where the people holding the sale just sit there and glare at you as you shop. I wanted people to be comfortable and feel welcome at my sale. Remember, you want them there—let them know they're welcome.

- Say "good morning" or "hello!" to everyone who comes to your sale. We were experiencing a heat wave the week during our sale last year, so we talked a lot about the weather. This is the time to make idle small talk . . . don't get personal . . . just greet them, smile, make a comment about the weather (or some other innocent remark), and maybe ask them if there's anything specific they're looking for. If someone comes and goes without buying anything, still thank them for stopping by and wish them a good day. Not only is it a nice thing to do, but other customers will overhear you and it'll make them more comfortable too, knowing you're nice to everyone, not just buying customers.

- Consider providing coffee if it's a cold day (offer it free—for donation only) or ice cold lemonade if it's warm weather. Let your kids man the refreshment table. My daughter made some extra money for a future trip to Mexico she's planning with our church youth group by doing this at our sale.

- I personally think it's better to price things a little bit on the high side, rather than too low. If someone really wants an item that they feel is overpriced, they'll make an offer.

- Since I planned on doing another garage sale in the future, I didn't come down on my prices too much since everything that didn't sell would just find it's way into my next sale.

- If your goal is to clear out as much stuff as possible (and make a few pennies on the side), offer some sort of great deal on the afternoon of the last day such as: everything a customer can stuff into a shopping bag for $1, or half price on all items after 12 noon on Saturday, or freebies in the late afternoon of the final day.

CHAPTER EIGHTEEN

🍃 Homemade Alternatives 🍃

Here are some homemade alternatives to use around the house that can replace more expensive store bought items.

FABRIC SOFTENER: ½ cup white vinegar added during the rinse cycle of your washing machine.

GLASS CLEANER: 2 cups white vinegar mixed with water to make one gallon. Use in spray pump bottle.

DRAIN CLEANER: Pour ½ cup baking soda down the drain. Add ½ cup vinegar. Let sit for ten minutes, and then rinse with a kettle full of boiling water poured down the drain.

Homemade Laundry Liquid Recipe

One bar plain soap (no fragrance, additives, etc. Ivory soap is a good example.)

1 cup washing soda (not baking soda or Borax™)

Large plastic container (about 3 gallons) with lid

Fill plastic container with hot tap water. Set aside. Grate bar of soap into saucepan. Add cold water to cover. Heat until soap is dissolved, stirring constantly. Add soap mixture to hot water in bucket. Stir to combine. Add one cup washing soda and stir (IMPORTANT: be sure you add the washing soda AFTER you stir the soap mixture into the bucket of hot water). Cool. The bucket of soap mixture will turn into a white gelatin-like soap as it cools (it might not thicken into much more than a runny, soupy mess, but it's still usable at that consistency).

To Use: Add one to two cups to a full load of laundry. Your clothes will come out clean with no scent. If you miss the scent of detergent, use half of a fabric softener sheet in the dryer. The homemade detergent doesn't foam or make suds, so don't worry if you were expecting suds and didn't see any. It's also best to use the smallest amount of laundry liquid as possible. Experiment a bit. Using too much can cause your clothes to look dingy if the soap isn't rinsed out fully. If you find your heavily soiled clothes need more help removing odor during the wash, add ½ cup white vinegar to the rinse cycle.

Also, if your white clothes start to look a bit dingy after using this homemade detergent, you can add one cup of dry non-chlorine bleach to the laundry liquid at the same time you stir in the washing soda.

**Washing soda in the USA is manufactured by Arm and Hammer™ and is sold with the other laundry additives (usually near the Borax™). Washing soda looks like a large box of baking soda.

Automatic Dishwasher Soap
In each detergent cup in the dishwasher, place two tablespoons EACH of Borax™ and baking soda. Wash as usual. I find the smell from the strong chemicals in regular dishwasher detergent bothers me, but I can use this recipe with no problems. It smells clean, but not from heavy chemicals.

Windshield Washer Solution
3 cups isopropyl alcohol
1 Tablespoon liquid dish detergent
10 cups water

Mix ingredients together. Use to fill your windshield washer reservoir on your vehicle. You can keep some handy in a spray bottle to spray car windows before scraping off ice.

Spa Milk Bath
2 cups salt
2 cups baking soda
2 cups nonfat dry milk
Mix ingredients together. Store in airtight container.   To use, add one cup to warm bath water.

Facial Mask
1 cup finely chopped oatmeal (whirl in the blender briefly)
1 container live-culture plain (non-flavored) yogurt
½ cup lemon juice
Mix oatmeal with yogurt; stir in lemon juice. Apply to clean, dry skin on face and neck. Leave on skin for 15 - 20 minutes. Rinse with warm water. Pat dry.

Fizzing Bath Bombs
2 tablespoons cornstarch
2 tablespoons citric acid (sold as Fruit Fresh in the US)
¼ c. baking soda
3 tablespoon coconut oil
½ teaspoon fragrance oil (your choice)
In bowl, mix together cornstarch, citric acid and baking soda. Melt coconut oil and add fragrance. Slowly drizzle oils into powder mixture. Mix well. Scoop out by scant ¼ cup, roll into balls. Let sit for 2 - 3 hours, and check to see if the balls have lost their shape. Reshape if necessary. Let dry for 48 hours. Wrap in clear plastic wrap, or colored wrap for gift giving. To use, just place in bath as water fills tub.

A Simple Choice

Part Five
🍃 Simple Family Fun 🍃

CHAPTER NINETEEN
🍃 Simplify the Holidays 🍃

"And it was always said of him, that he knew how to keep Christmas well, if any man alive possessed the knowledge. May that be truly said of . . . all of us!" —Charles Dickens, *A Christmas Carol*

When the holidays are right around the corner, we often hear the wonderful sounds of our favorite carols and seasonal music. But too many of us tend to sing different words to the familiar tune of Jingle Bells:

Dashing to the mall, in a light blue mini-van,
Stashing all our loot, behind the garbage can.
We think the kids need more, 'though their closet's full of junk,
Then someone gives unneeded things we'll just stow into a trunk!
      Ohhhh . . .
Christmas bills! Christmas bills! For Christmas we must pay!
See all of our Christmas bills
Still here on New Year's Day! Hey . . .
Christmas bills! Christmas bills! We can't pay today . . .
We have so many Christmas bills,
There's got to be a better way . . .

Do the phrases, "frugal living" and "holiday giving," seem to be at opposite ends of the spending spectrum? Is it possible to spend no more in December than during other months of the year? Will your family still love you if they don't find "the latest and the greatest" under the tree?

Our families deserve the best we can give. But if we're paying our Christmas debts for the next five years, complete with all the stresses that usually accompany outstanding bills, what good is it? No matter what our personal financial situation, we all could use a few simple, money-saving ideas for the holidays.

TRY CHECKING OUT BOOKS FROM THE LIBRARY ON HOLIDAY CUSTOMS AND CRAFTS FROM OTHER LANDS. These books can provide a wealth of innovative ideas, often for minimal expense. One year, in a book on Swedish customs, we found instructions for making an evergreen Advent wreath. Old newspapers soaked in water and wrapped around a wire coat hanger, were decorated with pine boughs from a backyard tree. Four large nails that stuck through the paper wreath held the candles, and we added finishing touches of small pine cones and red bows. The Advent wreath was beautiful, incredibly simple and made from items found around the house. It also added a meaningful centerpiece to our holiday celebrations.

DO YOU HAVE SOLID COLORED GLASS ORNAMENTS THAT YOU'RE TIRED OF? Let your children decorate them with glitter glue, holiday stickers or craft paints. This tip serves a dual purpose: new decorations for very little money, and an inexpensive, fun holiday activity for the whole family!

HOW ABOUT GIVING A HOMEMADE "DESSERT-OF-THE-MONTH" GIFT CERTIFICATE TO SOMEONE SPECIAL ON YOUR GIFT LIST? Or maybe a "Cookie-of-the-Month," or "Dinner-of-the-Month?" Each month you would deliver a different, home-baked goody to the lucky recipient. This gift is especially enjoyed by people who might not eat a lot of home-cooking, i.e. college students, singles, elderly shut-ins. These are also appreciated greatly by moms with multiple-children. (A treat they didn't have to prepare? They'll be so thankful for your thoughtfulness!)

LEARN TO DO CALLIGRAPHY. IT'S MUCH EASIER THAN IT LOOKS. You can make personalized gifts by doing calligraphy for the person's name and then framing it in a simple mat with a pressed flower or two glued to the picture or mat. You can also decorate a framed calligraphy graphic of a favorite quote, poem or scripture verse.

DO YOU ENJOY SENDING HOLIDAY CARDS BUT THE PRICE OF STORE-BOUGHT CARDS IS MAKING THIS TRADITION ALMOST IMPOSSIBLE? Make your own cards by decorating card stock with rubber stamps, pressed flowers or calligraphy. Better yet, make your own personalized holiday postcards, and save on postage, as well. For making your own "recycled" postcards, neatly trim off the front cover of old holiday cards. Turn the card over and position it horizontally. On the back, draw a straight line down the middle of the card. Stamp and fill it out like you would a regular post-card with the address on the right-hand side and your brief message on the left. You can also make postcards by purchasing card stock at your local office supply store and cutting the 8.5" by 11" sheets into four squares and then decorating the front side with rubber stamps. This is extremely economical as 500 sheets (which would make 2000 postcards) will only cost you about $8.00. You can also make postcards from any greeting cards (not just holiday cards) to send throughout the year.

FOR BEAUTIFUL, INEXPENSIVE GIFT WRAP WITH A COUNTRY-LOOK, SPONGE PAINT THE PLAIN SIDE OF FLATTENED PAPER GROCERY BAGS WITH GREEN, RED OR WHITE TEMPERA PAINT. Use various holiday shapes (trees, stars, candy canes, etc.). Tie the wrapped gifts with plain raffia or twine. The finished product is rustic, yet very elegant! This is another dual purpose tip: money-saver and fun—but somewhat messy—activity for the family.

DO YOU TAKE LOTS OF PHOTOGRAPHS AND NEVER KNOW WHAT TO DO WITH ALL THOSE EXTRA PRINTS? Small photo albums with nice snapshots of your children taken throughout the year make great gifts for grandpar-ents. Also, an album with current photos of various extended family members is a welcome gift for out-of-town relatives who can't make it home for the holidays. Small, plastic photo albums can often be found at variety stores for less than two dollars.

FOR LARGE FAMILIES AT THE HOLIDAYS, PUT THE NAME OF EACH PERSON OR FAMILY GROUP INTO A HAT. Draw names. The name you draw is the only one you buy a gift for that year. Be sure to set a reasonable spending limit.

LIMIT YOUR GIFT LIST. Contact your gift giving circle and chances are good that you have friends, neighbors, co-workers or extended family who would love to cut back on their own gift giving this year as well.

HARD TO SHOP FOR PEOPLE (teenagers, in-laws, etc.) appreciate a gift certificate to their favorite clothing or music store, or a subscription to a magazine dealing with their hobbies or personal interests.

STOCK UP AT END-OF-THE-SEASON SALES ON GIFT WRAP, GIFT BOXES, RIBBON AND CARDS. Look for Christmas wrap without Christmas motifs that can be used year round (solid colors, stripes, abstract designs). Don't forget during the year to check for sales on wrapping supplies on the day after various commercialized holidays like Valentine's Day, Easter and Mother's Day. You can often find beautiful wrappings that were intended for a particular holiday but don't have any tell-tale decorations that would limit their use.

HAVE A CHRISTMAS CAROLING PARTY. INVITE EVERYONE BACK TO YOUR HOUSE FOR COOKIES AND HOT SPICED CIDER OR HOT COCOA. This is a great way to have fun, build community spirit with your neighbors, include people of all ages and also get outside for a couple of fun-filled hours.

HOST A COOKIE EXCHANGE FOR FRIENDS AND NEIGHBORS EARLY IN THE HOLIDAY SEASON. Everyone bakes 6 - 10 dozen of only one cookie recipe, but they come home with a wonderful variety of festive cookies. This saves everyone money on baking since you only need to purchase the ingredients for one recipe and can consequently purchase some ingredients in bulk. As the hostess, you only need to provide beverages and your own cookies. As an outreach in keeping with the season of giving, each person could bring an extra dozen cookies. The extras would then be donated to a shut-in, a homeless shelter or a family experiencing a crisis. I remember one year my daughter unexpectedly had to have surgery in mid-December. Between running around constantly from doctor, to x-rays, to lab and then her recovery time after the surgery, I had no time to do any special holiday baking that year. It would've been lovely if someone had dropped off a couple dozen home-baked cookies in the midst of our holiday stress. I now look for opportunities like that to be of help, especially around the holidays when we can get so busy and caught up in our own plans that we forget about how difficult it can be for families who are experiencing unusually stressful events through the holidays.

AN INEXPENSIVE ACTIVITY WE OFTEN DO IS TO HAVE A CHRISTMAS PICNIC LUNCH AT A LOCAL PARK. Just getting outside in the fresh air is a welcome relief in the midst of the indoor activities of the holiday. We live in Washington state where December weather isn't usually considered picnic weather, but that's actually part of the fun. On several occasions, we've bundled up in multiple layers of coats and hats, and then sat at a picnic table eating hot soup and sandwiches while drinking cocoa or hot spiced cider. We also brought a few snacks to share with the squirrels and birds that came out to see what on earth our family was doing in their park on such a cold and blustery day.

COLLECT FAVORITE RECIPES FROM ASSORTED FAMILY MEMBERS AND THEN PUT TOGETHER A FAMILY COOKBOOK TO GIVE AS GIFTS. This can be done simply, just hand write the recipes on file cards and bind together. A more elaborate version can be done on a computer and either stapled into a booklet or taken to a local printer for comb-binding. I've discovered that making booklets usually costs less than $2 a piece (depending on the number of pages and size and quality of the paper used), but I've had to call around to find the best prices. You can also ask people to carefully hand write their favorite recipes—maybe including a funny story about the recipe or sharing a bit about it's history and then photocopy the originals and bind them all together. These make welcome gifts for friends and family.

OTHER SIMPLE, HOMEMADE GIFT IDEAS: candles are easy gifts, especially beeswax ones; make a gift basket of home canned items (jellies, fruit, sauces, pie fillings); cookies; homemade cloth wine-bags with a favorite bottle of wine; decorative painted trays; homemade bath salts; homemade coffee, tea, cocoa and dry soup mixes; fresh flowers and garden bouquets; homemade breads and muffins. One nice thing about giving consumable gifts is that you won't be forcing additional clutter onto someone else in the form of gifts. Two important things to remember about giving homemade gifts: 1) they can complicate your life if you're not careful, and 2) many times they're not appreciated by people who expect store-bought gifts. Don't expect too much from yourself, and don't sacrifice spending time with your family just for saving a few pennies. I've known people who have spent the entire holiday season stressing out over making the "perfect" homemade gifts, rather than relaxing and enjoying their family, friends and other favorite holiday activities.

Careful stewardship of our resources during the holidays doesn't have to mean deprivation and joylessness. Spend time this year prayerfully identifying your personal priorities for your family during the holiday season.

When your children have grown and moved on to start holiday traditions of their own, will they remember the gripe sessions their parents had over the stack of past-due Christmas bills? Or will they treasure the memories of quiet times of family togetherness and joy throughout the Advent season? Will they look back with reverence to a time spent in close communion with their Creator, thankfulness for His gifts and heightened awareness of the true meaning of Christmas? Or will they focus on the crazy times each year when mom flew through the house, cleaning wildly and snapping at everyone in sight because everything needed to be "perfect" before the guests arrived?

Simple, thoughtful and purposeful living can bring clearer focus to our daily lives, and added meaning and joy to our family celebrations.

If you want more ideas for simplifying your holidays, read the wonderful book, *Unplug the Christmas Machine: A Complete Guide to Putting Love and Warmth Back Into the Season*, by Jo Robinson and Jean Coppock Staeheli. You can probably find this book at the library or you can order it through the inter-library loan system.

Mary Hunt's book, *Debt-Proof Your Holidays*, is also a helpful way to avoid the "after-the-holidays-debt-hangover" so many people experience.

CHAPTER TWENTY
🍃 Family Fun and Games 🍃

"Oh, the fun of arriving at a house and feeling the spark that tells you that you are going to have a goodtime."—Mark Hampton

Entertainment doesn't have to be expensive or complicated. Sometimes the simplest ideas are the most fun. While preparing for a birthday party for one of my children, I checked out several books from the library on party games, and also wracked my brain trying to remember fun group games from my own childhood. I came up with several fun ideas to use at the party and I'll share them here. Many of these games work equally well for children's parties, grown-up parties and mixed-age groups (such as family gatherings).

Keep a Straight Face
Two teams sit facing each other in two lines. One team is chosen to go first and they must keep a straight face no matter what. In the meantime, the opposing team is doing everything within their power to make the other team laugh or crack a smile. No touching or tickling, but other than that, anything goes! It's so funny to watch the creative ways people try to make each other laugh.

Spot the Thimble
Everyone leaves the room for a moment while one person hides a thimble somewhere in plain sight in the room. When the people who left the room return, they look for the thimble. As soon as they see the thimble they sit down without letting others know where the thimble's hiding.

The last one to find the thimble does a forfeit of some sort (i.e.: sings a song, recites a poem, spells their name backward, kisses their own shadow, etc.). The first one to see the thimble hides it on the next round.

Musical Spoons

This is played like Musical Chairs. You set out spoons on the floor (one less spoon than the number of players). As the music plays, everyone crawls around on the floor in time to the music. When the music stops, each person tries to grab a spoon. One person won't be able to, so they're out until the next game. Continue the game using one spoon less than the number of players until only one person is left.

Pig Pile Chairs

This game is a reversed version of Musical Chairs. For this game, you start with one less chair than the number of players in the group. Turn on music and have the players move around the chairs until the music stops. Then everyone needs to rush for a chair, but two children end up sitting on one chair. During each round, continue removing chairs. At the end of the game you'll have a Pig Pile of children on the one chair.

Noah's Ark

This game was the hit of my daughter's slumber party. The girls could've played it all night! Put the names of animals onto slips of paper and then into a hat (be sure to include two of each animal, of course). Let each participant draw an animal name but don't tell anyone else what it is. They're going to be the animals on Noah's Ark and something has happened so all the animals escaped from their pens. The animals now need to find their partners. The lights go out, and then everyone spreads throughout the room or throughout the house. Then they're told to find their "partners" by only making the noises of the animals.

At my daughter's party, at the end of the game, I purposely didn't use matches for any of the animal names so none of the children had a partner—but the girls didn't know this! My husband and I sat on the couch and laughed hysterically while all the little animals went mooing and barking and meowing all over the house looking for their non-existent partners.

Strike-a-Pose
This is a variation on the standard Charades game. Put words into a hat such as: tragic, shocked, love struck, smart, silly. The person who is "it" draws a word and then strikes a pose that somehow communicates the word (no acting out, just holding one pose).

Mannerisms
This is another Charades-type game. This time put slips of paper containing ADVERBS into a hat. In this game, people in the room ask "it" to do things to act out the word. The players say something like, "Go to the door in the manner of the word," or "Read a book in the manner of the word," or "Sit in the chair in the manner of the word." The person who figures out the word is "it" for the next round.

International Shopper
Come up with a list of items for the "shoppers" to purchase (i.e.: a pot of honey, ballet shoes, peanut butter, a pound of butter, an umbrella, a dog leash). The shopper draws an item from the list in a hat. The shopper isn't able to speak the language of the store owner, so he or she needs to act out the item they want to buy. The rest of the players try to guess what the shopper wants to purchase.

Build a Story
One person starts a story, any kind of story on any topic. When the first person is satisfied with his start, he "passes" to the next person, preferably stopping the telling in the middle of an exciting part. Then the next person adds onto the story in any way they want until he is ready to pass it on again. This can turn into a wild and imaginative story, taking

many imaginative twists and turns. Keep passing the story to anyone gathered around until someone chooses to end it.

Add a Drawing

Take a large piece of paper and take turns drawing. Someone starts with a background (examples: a forest, a meadow, a city street, the sky, another planet, etc.). The next person adds something to the picture: a castle, an airplane, a hut. The next person adds something else to the picture like a knight, a hamster or a dinosaur until a story starts to evolve in the drawing—the knight in front of a castle was fighting a dragon when suddenly a space alien appears in a UFO and returns the knight's dog who has been changed into an alien being. I think you get the idea. This is also a fairly quiet way to amuse children while waiting at the doctor's office or waiting for your food to arrive at the table in a restaurant.

Dozens of Family Fun Ideas

Having fun during school vacations or on weekends doesn't have to mean breaking the bank. I've definitely discovered that the simplest items found (for free!) around the house are many times the most fun for my three children. I've often watched them playing contentedly for hours with empty cardboard toilet paper tubes, plastic fly-swatters, sticks and twigs, rocks, bugs, empty boxes, paper grocery bags, assorted scraps of paper and other used office supplies. Sometimes I wonder why I've ever spent money to actually buy toys—I don't think any store-bought item has ever brought as many hours of creative play for my children as an empty shoe box.

For family entertainment, you might like to do a bit more than pulling out a few cardboard tubes, so here's a list of ideas for inexpensive family fun.

1) Attend outdoor concerts in local parks. Take a blanket or lawn chairs. Pack a lunch or dinner. Some parks set up big movie screens after dark for Moonlight Movies. Bring your own lawn chairs, blankets, popcorn and drinks.

2) Check the 'What's Happening' or 'Weekend' section of local newspapers for inexpensive or free family fun activities.

3) Take a stay-at-home vacation (write for tourist brochures—plan each day like you would a vacation that you went away on—get up early, pack a lunch, take in as many sites as you can).

4) Perform a family service project (pick up litter, volunteer at a soup kitchen, plant trees).

5) Volunteer at a zoo or nature center.

6) Do a casual unit study (pick a subject—i.e., ducks—learn about it at the library, take field trips, draw pictures, take photos, watch movies related to the subject, do crafts, write creative stories).

7) Call local manufacturing plants. Many will give your family or small group a free tour, plus any complimentary samples make great souvenirs.

8) Summer reading programs at local libraries offer great motivation for reading, and sometimes fun incentives such as coupons for local attractions, etc.

9) Buying an annual family pass to a local tourist or educational attraction (zoo, aquarium, whatever) pays for itself quickly—you can go back to the same place whenever you want a family outing (and then you don't feel rushed to "see it all" in one day when you know you'll be back again soon). Many have reciprocating privileges at zoos and/or museums all over the country. Buy a pass to a different park or attraction next year.

10) Discover the joy of Nature Walks. Take along hand-held magnifying glasses and/or binoculars.

11) Bird watching, camping, beach combing, bike riding, fishing, hiking, blowing bubbles.

12) Organize some group activities: Family Olympics (with several other families), Kids' Backyard Sleep-over, Progressive Dinner, Stargazing Night, Recycled Craft Party.

13) Pack a lunch and some balls, etc. Take to a park and play games.

14) Have a "meet the neighbors" picnic. Invite everyone to bring a potluck dish to share, and drinks and utensils for themselves.

15) Let the kids write/perform a circus or play, or put on an art exhibit of their handicrafts and art work from the school year. Invite grandparents, aunts, uncles. Serve popcorn and lemonade.

16) On hot days, play board games outside on a blanket in the shade of a tree.

17) Learn a new game, sport, or craft.

18) Give your little ones a bucket of plain water and a large clean paint brush. Let them "paint" the house, fence or sidewalk with water.

19) Play whiffle ball instead of baseball. Even the little ones can join in.

20) Sleep under the stars in your backyard and identify the constellations.

21) Have your children attend a week of Vacation Bible School at a local church.

22) Take your kids out for an appetizer and pop instead of a full meal. Or just go out for dessert.

23) Go fly a kite . . . literally!

24) Have a family music festival, concert or recital.

25) Play old card games (the games are new to your children!).

26) If you're stuck in the car for a long time, try this: look for something odd and out of place lying along the road (maybe an old boot beside the highway), and then take turns making up stories about how it

came to be there (everything from an alien attack to a flood disaster scenario is possible).

27)Have a scavenger hunt.

28) Have theme nights. Example: for "Spy Night" you could watch Harriet the Spy, make up Spy Kits, and play a spy game like Flashlight Tag. Or have Science-Fiction night: watch an old science-fiction movie like War of the Worlds and then a modern one like Independence Day (very similar basic plot—possible end of the world due to alien invasion). Talk about how sci-fi has changed, and stayed the same, in the past few decades.

29) Give your kids their own small section of the garden to plant whatever they want: flowers, vegetables. Make gardening a family event.

30) Go berry picking. Make something yummy out of the berries you pick (jam, cobbler, smoothies). You can also freeze berries individually on a cookie sheet and then place them frozen into a plastic bag for hot weather snacking.

31) Recall fond memories from your own childhood that you can recreate with your own children: catching fireflies, fishing, hay rides, swinging on rope swings, building tree houses, picking wildflowers, making ice cream, playing checkers. Also, give some thought to what our ancestors did for entertainment. They knew how to have fun without spending a lot of money.

32) Start a collection: rocks, pressed flowers, leaves, feathers.

33) Go to a Farmer's Market.

34) Have a water fight or run through the sprinkler (or just spray your kids with a hose while they run through the yard).

35) Many museums and local attractions have free days regularly (i.e.: first Thursday of the month, etc.). Call and ask.

36) Things to make: bubbles, tie-dye (socks are fun and relatively inexpensive), paper mache, sand clay, homemade paper, sidewalk chalk, kites, pinwheels, pressed flowers, pressed flower crafts (cards, pictures,

candles), daisy chains, butter, frozen treats. Recipes and instructions for some of these ideas included in chapter twenty-two.

CHAPTER TWENTY-ONE

🍃 Nature Connections 🍂

"Nature-study cultivates in the child the love of the beautiful; it brings to him early a perception of color, form and music... he reads the music score of the bird . . . and the patter of the rain, the gurgle of the brook, the sighing of the wind in thepine."—Anna Botsford Comstock, *Handbook of Nature Study*

When asked what activities bring great satisfaction, many people responded that anything outdoors or involving being in touch with the natural environment creates joy and a feeling of contentment.

Our family hasn't been blessed with acres of property off in the country for our children to frolic in to their heart's content. But a small city lot and many local parks have offered us tremendous opportunities for outdoor nature activities.

To make up for the lack of open natural space in our neighborhood, we go to various local parks at least two to three times per week. We don't go to the parks for the play equipment but for the exposure to a more natural setting. We are about half-an-hour driving time from Puget Sound so we often frequent parks with direct beach access. When the tide's out, the kids explore tide pools, find crabs and enjoy the fresh salt air. Digging in the sand and making castles and roadways is always fun, too!

There is a "wilderness" park in our town which has access to a river bank, several walking trails through undisturbed woods and a big open field for playing and running.

Observations

Last year, we started bringing the children's Nature Notebooks whenever we went to the wilderness park. Nature Notebooks are artist sketchbooks where the children can draw whatever natural items strike their fancy.

Throughout the fall, we revisited the wilderness park once each week and kept track of the changes we observed as the season progressed. Everything was green and full of leaves, at first. Then we saw the gradual change of colors, until finally, after an early snow storm, the trees were bare and the ground covered with leaves.

We casually discussed the difference between deciduous and evergreen trees and the kids really saw firsthand what that means. At first, the evergreens were barely visible amongst the heavy foliage. After the autumn leaves were gone, the evergreens were the only observable green in the woods. The kids also noticed on their own that the level of the river had gradually gone down over the several months we'd been observing it.

We watched a large group of mushrooms spring up and practically overrun a section of the park's grass. The kids had great fun sketching the odd-looking mushrooms with their funny little caps. "They're like little umbrellas, Mom!"

One day, my ten-year-old daughter sat entranced by a Black-Capped Chickadee darting between the branches of an Autumn-clad maple. Although she had her Nature Notebook with her, the busy little bird just wasn't cooperating and holding still for his portrait.

When we arrived home, my daughter ran to the bookcase and grabbed a bird identification book. After looking up Chickadees, she used the illustration in the book as the model for the sketch she then added to her Nature Notebook. She also drew in a background of the various trees we had seen at the park.

Backyard Bird Survey

Another nature activity we've participated in right in our own small yard is the Backyard Bird Survey sponsored by the Washington State Department of Fish and Wildlife. I know that many other states offer similar programs, so if you're interested, contact your local Department of Fish and Wildlife to find out more.

Here is how the Backyard Bird Survey works: we do a bird count in our yard for a two hour stretch of time twice during each two week observation period. This surveying goes on throughout the winter months.

By participating in the Survey, we've learned a great deal about bird identification, and the children have actually started bird-watching at other times and in other places. The binoculars have become a favorite "toy."

One time during our survey hours, we saw a Sharp-Shinned Hawk snatch a small House Finch off our feeder. Rather traumatic, especially since the hawk ate its meal in an open tree within our line of sight, but a much better learning experience than the best wildlife drama on television!

I want to encourage those of you who might not have easy access to your own fields and forests, there are other readily available opportunities for outdoor play and learning activities.

I can't stress enough how valuable I've found the Nature Notebook idea to be. We are going to start taking our notebooks (I keep one, too) with us whenever we go on any sort of outdoor adventure. Even trips to the local zoo can be enriched by taking a sketchbook. My understanding of the Nature Notebook idea, however, is that it should only contain sketches of objects the child has actually seen firsthand in natural settings. Zoo trips would require a separate "Zoo Notebook."

Nature Notebook

A love for the natural world begins when an item seen firsthand sparks an interest in the child. When a grinning, dirt-smudged toddler brings an earthworm in from the garden and proclaims, "Look, mommy . . . a snake!" a true naturalist has been born. A deep acquaintance with the natural world can cultivate the power of accurate observation, an important skill in future scientific endeavors. Exploring nature inspires the child to ask questions about cause and effect, and also leads to the discovery of the inter-connectedness of living things and the environment.

Charlotte Mason, an educator in England in the previous century, advocated the use of Nature Notebooks as a vital part of each child's education and an important ingredient for personal growth. These notebooks were the ongoing record of firsthand nature experiences, containing drawings with labels, nature-related poetry and prose, weather notations and whatever else interested the individual child. The notebooks were voluntary projects; not an assignment from the teacher. In the book, *Handbook of Nature Study* by Anna Botsford Comstock, the author recommends keeping a field notebook. Comstock says, "these books, of whatever quality, are precious beyond price to their owners. And why not? For they represent what cannot be bought or sold—personal experience in the happy world of out-of-doors."

To inspire your children with the idea of creating a personal Nature Notebook, try keeping one yourself as a hobby and for personal enrichment. There's no better teacher than the example set by an enthusiastic and involved parent. A blank spiral-bound artist sketchbook and some high quality drawing pencils are the main tools you'll need to start a field diary. Also accurate and easy-to-use field guides are helpful for identifying plants and animals; and binoculars or a high-power hand-held magnifying glass add an extra dimension to your field observations.

If you're thinking, "I can't do this . . . I have no artistic ability," don't let that thought stop you from considering this idea. The book, *Drawing With Children*, by Mona Brookes, is a simple way to learn basic drawing techniques for both children and art-inhibited adults.

Even if you're not currently living in a rural setting surrounded by natural environments, you can make use of Nature Notebooks in your own backyard or local parks. Drawings of trees, flowers, leaves, birds, butterflies, earthworms, rocks, insects and even the child's own pets are possible no matter where you live. Keeping a detailed personal Nature Diary can become an enjoyable, educational and rewarding hobby lasting a lifetime.

For those who might be interested in using this technique as an activity in a classroom or home school, remember that Nature Notebooks should be considered the personal property of the owner and never graded. Spelling, grammar and graphic drawings in the notebooks should be free from criticism or correction.

The more options available for inclusion in a Nature Diary, the more likely you'll find one or more ideas that spark your interest. Some possible ideas:

- 1. Information learned or observed from firsthand observation (not things learned from teaching, television or books).

- 2. Drawings of leaves, flowers, birds, insects, anything found in its natural setting.

- 3. Labels for drawings (English and Latin names if applicable).

- 4. Notations on where the object was found.

- 5. Notations about the temperature or weather conditions, dates, etc.

- 6. Life cycles of plants. Draw the bare tree in winter; then the spring buds; the summer blooms; and finally the fall colors and seed pods. Or in a backyard garden draw a seed, then the sprouting seedling, then the full grown plant; draw the stem, leaves, flower, etc.; then draw the new seeds for starting the cycle over once again.

- 7. Draw and describe the activity of an ant hill or bird's nest.

- 8. Using a magnifying glass, draw the intricate details of a bee or butterfly wing (or any other fascinating object viewed under magnification).

- 9. Notations on the rising and setting times of the sun; sketches of the sun's position in the sky throughout the year and/or the phases of the moon.

- 10. Press and mount leaves or dried flowers.

- 11. Samples or drawings of different leaf types: divided; heart-shaped; fluted; needles.

- 12. Samples or drawings of different seeds: nuts; seed pods; seeds that fall to the ground; seeds that float through the air.

- 13. Parts of the flower: petal, sepal, stamen, etc.

- 14. Sketches of animal tracks (identify and label).

- 15. Sketches of the life cycles of animals. Caterpillar to cocoon to moth; egg to tadpole to frog (or salamander).

- 16. Nature-related poems or quotes. The poems can be discovered during the child's reading time, or include originally composed poems and prose.

- 17. A list of animal species seen firsthand (types of birds, mammals, fish, insects). Bird-watching hobbyists often keep a personal Bird List, a record of the species of birds they've seen over the course of their lives.

CHAPTER TWENTY-TWO
🍂 Homemade Alternatives 🍂

Making Homemade Paper
Supply List:

blender

warm water

scraps of old paper torn into small pieces (Soft, thick paper like construction paper works great. You can also include dryer lint, but don't use dryer lint ONLY, since it won't give your paper enough body.)

plain wooden picture frame (8"x10")

piece of window screen material (12"x14" or larger)

staple gun or waterproof glue

two large plastic dish pans or baby bathtubs

clean rags (at least 15"x15" square)

old newspapers

a rolling pin

metal shears to cut the screen

Optional: spray starch, iron

Place the torn scraps of paper and warm water into a large pan to soak until saturated and soft (the resulting paper pulp mixture is called "slurry"). Meanwhile, stretch the screen over the picture frame and staple screen to the frame. Scoop out one cup of slurry, put into blender and add water to fill blender. (If you want pure white paper, add ¼ cup chlorine bleach at this point.) Blend for a few seconds until it's smooth and mushy. Pour paper mush into large tub. Repeat several times until there's about 5 inches of mushy water in the tub.

For texture and color in your paper, you can now add to the paper mush in the tub: finely shredded corn husks, fine sawdust, crumbled or whole dry leaves, dry grass, shredded dry onion skins, grated dry fruit skins, dry flower petals. Be creative. Dip the screened picture frameunder the mush; then holding the frame level, shift it back and forth until a layer of mush settles evenly over the surface. This layer should be about ½ inch thick.

Without tilting frame, lift frame and mush layer out of the dishpan. Hold over the pan to allow the water to drain out. If the mush clumps together or there are holes, put the frame back under the mush layer in the dishpan and start again. (The mush left on the frame is called "wet leaf.")

Place a clean rag over the top of the drained wet leaf. Press down gently, squeezing out more water. Lay a few pieces of old newspaper down onto a table. Carefully turn the frame, wet paper, and rag upside down onto the newspaper, and CAREFULLY lift off frame. Cover the wet paper with another rag. (You now have a sandwich of two rags with a layer of wet paper between).

Roll the rag/paper sandwich with a rolling pin to press out more water. You can sandwich the rag/paper between small stacks of newspaper and continue pressing with rolling pin to remove more water.

Carefully peel off the top rag. Turn the wet paper and bottom rag over onto either a smooth counter top or a piece of glass (paper side down), and then CAREFULLY peel off the remaining rag.

Let the paper dry overnight or longer.

If you want smooth paper, spray the dry paper with spray laundry starch until slightly damp; put a clean smooth rag over the damp paper, and iron with a slightly warm iron until the paper is dry. The starch will make the paper better for writing on, too.

You can use your homemade paper to make cards, wrap small gifts, cover a handmade book, write notes. Have fun!

Craft Dough Recipe

2 cups flour

1 cup salt

1 cup cold water

Mix ingredients together and knead until it becomes a medium stiff dough. Add more flour or water to adjust consistency if needed. To color, add several drops of food coloring and knead until mixed thoroughly. Store unused clay in sealed plastic bags in the refrigerator. Use as modeling clay, or roll out like cookie dough and cut with a cookie cutter. To make ornaments, bake on cookie sheet at 225 degrees for about one hour, or until it feels hard to the touch. Cool on wire rack. To protect your clay creations, dip in melted paraffin or coat with polyurethane.

Bubbles

5 cups water

½ cup liquid Joy dishwashing detergent

2 Tablespoons glycerin (found at drug stores)

Add dish soap and glycerin to pan of water. Stir gently to mix— don't let suds build up.

Crazy Crayons

Crayons (unwrapped and broken into pieces)

Pan spray

Glass jars (baby food jars work well)

Saucepan

Metal muffin tin or plastic candy molds

If you're using muffin tins, place several crayon pieces directly into each hole of the muffin tin. You can make the new crayons all one color, or mix complimentary colors to add interest. Heat the muffin tin in a 325 degree oven for five minutes (or until crayon bits are melted). Check frequently. Cool. Pop out of muffin tins.

To make crayons in plastic candy molds, place several pieces of crayon into each jar. Spray the candy molds with pan spray. Place the glass jar into saucepan, adding enough water to the pan to cover the jar halfway. Heat the pan over low heat until the crayons have melted. Watch constantly. Carefully pour the melted crayon into the candy molds. Let the crayons cool and pop them out of the molds.

Soap Crayons

1 ¾ cups Ivory Snow™ powder
¼ cup water
50 drops food coloring
Ice cube tray (or plastic candy molds)

Mix together soap powder and water. Add food coloring. Stir. Pour mixture into ice cube tray. Allow crayons to harden. Pop the crayons out of the tray and use to write in the bathtub.

Homemade Stickers

Assorted paper pictures (cut from magazines)
Scissors
Small bowl
White glue
White vinegar
Paintbrush or cotton swabs
Wax paper

Combine two parts glue and one part vinegar in bowl. Stir well. Brush a thin layer of glue mixture onto the back of each cut out with a paint brush or cotton swab, making sure to cover all the edges. Place the stickers on a sheet of wax paper and allow to air dry completely for about an hour. (Any flavor of powdered gelatin dessert mixed with a small amount of water can also be used for the "glue" to paint on the back of the stickers (tastes great for licking the stickers!)

Sidewalk Chalk

Plaster of Paris

A Simple Choice

Warm water

Powdered tempra paint

Molds (small cardboard tubes, trays that manicotti comes in, plastic candy molds, paper cups, cupcake liners, anything you can either pop the chalk out of or peel away from the finished chalk)

Mix the plaster of Paris according to package directions (using warm water). The consistency should be thick, but still pourable. Add a small amount of powdered paint (if desired), and then pour into molds. Let harden 48 hours.

APPENDIX A

 Recommended Resources

Financial Counseling

Consumer Credit Counseling Service
A nationwide nonprofit credit counseling service with over 1,200 local offices. Call 1-800-388-CCCS for the office near you.

Contact your local Better Business Bureau for names of other nonprofit credit counseling services in your area.

Christian Financial Concepts
Attn: Counseling Department
601 Broad Street SE
Gainesville, GA 30501
Financial advice from a biblical perspective. Include a self-addressed stamped envelope when you write.

Books

Debt Related
Debt Proof Your Holidays by Mary Hunt. Whether you're just looking for further frugal ideas for the upcoming holiday season, or you're truly dreading another after-holidays debt hangover, this book will be beneficial.

The Cheapskate Monthly Money-Makeover by Mary Hunt. How to get out of debt and stay that way! I highly recommend this book if you're currently experiencing difficulties with consumer debt. The author's personal story of overcoming $100,000 in consumer debt is inspiring to those struggling under the weight of indebtedness.

The Debt Squeeze by Ron Blue. How your family can become financially free (Christian perspective).

How to Get Out of Debt, Stay Out of Debt, and Live Prosperously by Jerrold Mundis. This book is by the founder of Debtors Anonymous.

Life After Debt by Bob Hammond. How to repair your credit and get out of debt once and for all.

Master Your Money by Ron Blue. A step-by-step plan for financial freedom (Christian perspective).

General Finance
The Financially Confident Woman by Mary Hunt. Nine habits that help build financial security (an excellent book regardless of your gender).

The Nine Steps to Financial Freedom by Suze Orman.

Frugal Living (Practical how-to advice)
The Best of the Cheapskate Monthly by Mary Hunt. Selected articles and tips from the popular Cheapskate Monthly newsletter.

The Best of Living Cheap News by Larry Roth. Practical advice on saving money and living well.

The Complete Cheapskate by Mary Hunt. How to break free from money worries forever.

Frugal Families by Jonni McCoy. Making the most of your hard earned money.

The Millionaire Next Door by Thomas Stanley and William Denko. The bestseller detailing the surprisingly frugal secrets of America's wealthy.

Miserly Moms by Jonni McCoy. Practical steps for living well on a limited budget.

Penny Pinching by Lee and Barbara Simmons. How to lower your everyday expenses without lowering your standard of living.

The Penny-Pinching Hedonist by Shel Horowitz. How to live like royalty with a peasant's pocketbook.

Raising Kids with Just a Little Cash by Lisa Reid.

Saving Money Any Way You Can, by Mike Yorkey. How to become a frugal family (Christian perspective).

Shattering the Two-Income Myth by Andy Dappen. Daily readings teaching how to live well on a single income. Great for families considering making the switch to a one income situation.

The Tightwad Gazette (Books One, Two and Three) by Amy Dacyczyn. These books are often nicknamed "The Frugal Bible." If you don't own all three, you're missing some important frugal tips and ideas. The first time I read one of these books, I put two of their simple tips into use—and immediately began saving our family $50 per month ($600 per year!). Not a bad return investment on a book I checked out from the library.

Tiptionary by Mary Hunt. A thorough collection of money saving tips organized according to subject matter. Great resource and easy to use.

1,001 Ways to Cut Your Expenses by Jonathan Pond. Pond really knows how to cut expenses, and he clearly and simply shares his expertise with readers.

Simple Living (more philisophical)
The Circle of Simplicity by Cecile Andrews. A guidebook for forming "Voluntary Simplicity" study groups.

Finding Focus in a Whirlwind World by Jean Flemming. Finding the focus for your life by identifying spiritual priorities (Christian perspective).

Gift from the Sea by Anne Morrow Lindbergh. Inspiring book on simplifying and finding focus in a woman's busy life.

Living More With Less by Doris Janzen Longacre. The classic simple living book. Well worth reading!

Choosing Simplicity: Real People Finding Peace and Fulfillment in a Complex World, by Linda Breen Pierce. Based on a landmark survey of over 200 people who have actively chosen a simpler lifestyle. A glimpse into the different ways various people are applying the concept of simplicity in their lives. A great book!

Living the Simple Life by Elaine St. James. A guide to scaling down and enjoying more.

Margin by Richard A. Swenson, MD. Restoring emotional, physical, financial, and time reserves to overloaded lives.

A Place Called Simplicity by Claire Cloninger. "The quiet beauty of simple living. . . ." This is a wonderful book. It inspired me more than anything else I've read on the subject of simplifying your life (Christian perspective).

The Simple Living Guide by Janet Luhrs

Simplify Your Life by Elaine St. James. 100 ways to slow down and enjoy more.

Simplify Your Life With Kids by Elaine St. James. 100 ways to make family life easier.

'Tis a Gift to be Simple by Barbara Sorensen. Embracing the freedom of living with less.

Unplug the Christmas Machine: Putting Joy Back into the Holiday by Jo Robinson. Don't wait until Christmas to read this book! The earlier you start thinking about the holidays, the easier it will be to make any necessary changes in your celebrations.

Your Money or Your Life by Joe Dominguez and Vicki Robin. Transforming your relationship with money. This book has been changing the lives and spending habits of people all over the world. A classic!

365 TV-Free Activities You Can Do With Your Child by Steven J. Bennet.

Cooking

Frozen Assets: How to Cook for a Day and Eat for a Month by Deborah Taylor-Hough. Less time in the kitchen means more time for activities you really enjoy. This book will show you a step-by-step plan to simplify and revolutionize the way you cook. Save time, save money, save your sanity!

Cheapskate in the Kitchen by Mary Hunt. Learn to prepare gourmet meals for a fraction of the cost of restaurant dining. I contributed several recipes to this book so you know it's got to be good.

Eat Healthy for $50 a Week by Rhonda Barfield. Yes, it really is possible to feed your family healthy meals for $50 per week (recipes included).

Homemade to Go by Mary Wells and Dee Bower. The complete guide to co-op cooking. Simplify meal preparation by sharing your cooking with friends during the week.

More-With-Less Cookbook by Doris Janzen Longacre. Helpful and thought provoking book published by the Mennonites. Every kitchen needs this cookbook on the shelf.

Home Organization

Clutter's Last Stand by Don Aslett.

Confessions of an Organized Homemaker by Deneice Schofield.

If I Could Just Get Organized by Karen Jogerst. Home management help for pilers and filers. To order, send $12.95 + $2.00 shipping and handling to: Rubies Publishing, P.O. Box 409, Manhattan MT 59741.

Is There Life After Housework by Don Aslett.

Kitchen Organization Tips by Deneice Schofield.

Simply Organized by Connie Coz and Cris Evatt.
  Unclutter Your Home by Donna Smallin.

Self-Sufficient Living

Back to Basics by Reader's Digest Books. How to learn and enjoy traditional American skills (buying land, building homesteads, alternative energy, raising food, canning, baking, cooking, metalworking, weaving, leatherwork, soapmaking, and much more).

The Encyclopedia of Country Living by Carla Emery. How to cultivate a garden, buy land, bake bread, raise farm animals, make sausage, milk a goat, grow herbs, churn butter, catch a pig, make soap, work with bees and more.

How to Develop a Low-Cost Family Food Storage System, by Anita Evangelista. Life is unpredictable. A sudden downturn in family finances can make food purchasing difficult. A severe storm can keep your family trapped at home for days. This book can help even the most financially strapped family learn to store emergency essentials.

Making the Best of Basics by James Talmadge Stevens. Chapters on storing and using everything from water, wheat, and dried fruits and vegetables to vitamin supplements to maintain your family's health, and emergency sources of fuel and energy. Includes over 200 recipes.

Where There is No Doctor: A Village Health Care Handbook by David Werner. A classic book enjoyed by Peace Corps workers and missionaries worldwide. Helpful information for anyone who lives in locations removed from immediate medical services.

Miscellaneous Books

The Stay-at-Home Mom's Guide to Making Money at Home by Liz Folger. Are you thinking of staying home full-time with your children, but still need some additional income? This book could provide the answers you're looking for.

The Single Parent Resource by Brook Noel with Art Klein. What kind of help do single parents need most in their day-to-day lives? The authors asked that question to over 500 single parents—and here are the answers never before available in a single guide.

Dirt Cheap Gardening: Hundreds of Ways to Save Money in Your Garden by Rhonda Massingham Hart. The author shares her years of practical experience and imaginative, time-tested ideas for saving money and cutting costs in the garden, and explains why some plants make better investments than others.

Women Leaving the Workplace by Larry Burkett. Help for women deciding to become stay-at-home parents (Christian perspective).

Newsletters

The Simple Times Email Newsletter / Editor, Deborah Taylor-Hough
A free e-mail newsletter for simple, frugal living—produced twice each month. To subscribe, send an e-mail with ANY message to: simple-times-subscribe@egroups.com
Web-page: http://members.aol.com/dsimple/times.html

The Cheapskate Monthly / Editor, Mary Hunt
PO Box 2135
Paramount, CA 90723-8135
Bringing dignity to the art of living within one's means. Excellent resource for anyone struggling with consumer debt.

Sample copy: Free with self-addressed stamped envelope
Web-page: http://www.cheapskatemonthly.com

Counting the Cost / Editor Nancy Twigg
7156 Peppermill Lane
Memphis, TN 38125
A bimonthly guide to adundant living without abundant spending.
Sample issue: $2
Web-page: http://www.countingthecost.com

The Dollar Stretcher / Editor, Gary Foreman
PO Box 23785
Fort Lauderdale, FL 33307
Sample issue: $1
Web-page: http://www.stretcher.com/

The Frugal Family Network Newsletter / Editors, Deana Ricks and Angie
Zalewski
PO Box 92731
Austin, TX 78709
Sample issue: Free with self-addressed stamped envelope
Web-page: http://www.frugalfamilynetwork.com

Web Resources
A Frugal, Simple Life
http://members.aol.com/dsimple/index.html
My web-pages for living the simple life.

Busy Cooks
http://busycooks.about.com/
Regular features on freezer meals, planned leftovers, quick cooking recipes, easy entertaining, and more.

The Dollar Stretcher
http://www.stretcher.com/
Web-site and e-mail newsletter with articles and tips for living frugally.

Frugal Family Network
http://frugalfamilynetwork.com/
Web-site and information about frugal living. Plus information about their print newsletter.

Miserly Moms
http://www.miserlymoms.com/
Web-page by Jonni McCoy, author of Miserly Moms and Frugal Families. Good information for stay-at-home parents.

APPENDIX B

🌿 Why Simplicity? 🌿

Why Simplicity?

While preparing this book, I sent out a questionnaire to people on my assorted mailing lists and on-line message boards. Over one hundred people responded to those questionnaires, and their thoughtful and sometimes thought-provoking answers provide a snapshot of what simplicity looks like in the lives of real people.

Some people have chosen to voluntarily simplify their lives for spiritual or emotional reasons while others were forced into a form of "involuntary" simplicity due to corporate lay-offs or unforeseen difficulties. Some down-shifted from high-paying, high-power, high-stress careers while others never chose that path to begin with, preferring to focus on simpler things from the start. Some were retired and already enjoying their grandchildren while others were young and just starting out on their own. Many were married with numerous children and many others were happily single with no children at all.

But whatever their financial background, age or lifestyle, over and over again the people responding to the questionnaire expressed a profound peace and joy discovered through the process of simplifying and focusing their lives on things other than the nine-to-five rat race or the quest for "newer, bigger, better."

This book couldn't be made big enough to handle all the responses received, but the following are a sampling of the reasons, lessons and practical steps real people have discovered on their personal paths to the simple life. My hope and prayer is that you'll meet kindred spirits in the pages that follow, people who can take you by the hand, offering inspiration and guidance for your own journey down the path toward simplicity.

"Simplicity means making deliberate choices; being aware of what I'm doing, seeing or saying instead of going through life on automatic pilot; treading lightly on the earth; not being possessed by my possessions; having an uncluttered spirit as well as an uncluttered home. I am making deliberate choices in that I am choosing to live with fewer possessions in order to have more peace of mind. I am trying to separate my wants from my needs and to reorder my priorities. I don't want to have to work at a job I hate just because I need the money to finance a lifestyle that isn't really making me happy. Simplicity gives me more peace of mind. I have less stuff to worry about being broken or stolen, less to dust and clean, more time to think of more important things like family and friends, and time to just 'be.'

"I've moved a lot in the past two years, including from one country to another, and it's made me re-evaluate what's important. I've been under considerable stress, often worrying about things being broken in the moves. Now I realize they are just things and if they are broken, it doesn't really matter. Simplicity is a concept I've only recently discovered, but I've made big steps in physically uncluttering my life. Now I'm working on the internal uncluttering. I hope to find inner peace, more contentment with what I have in my life, and less desire to keep up with others."

—Diane G., Indiana—Legal Secretary

"Simplicity means taking time to smell the flowers; realizing relationships are more important than acquiring things; understanding the value of frugality and financial independence and practicing those concepts; reducing clutter and helping the earth by living more lightly; not sweating over the details because life is too short to do so; working doing something you love that also leaves time for other outside pleasures and pursuits. I was motivated to live simply by realizing I don't want to work 80 hours a week, and that money is not very important. I want to pursue a meaningful career and have time for family also.

"I am hampered if I have a complicated lifestyle and am burdened by debt and arduous details. I became burned out while working for a corporation in its constant pursuit of making money at all costs. I found a better job (my current one) and moved on, after taking a vacation first. I wanted to change while I am still young, and not ask 'what if' when I am older. My pursuit of more meaningful legal work (staff attorney for judges) has meant less money, but not a sacrifice due to my enjoyment of it.

"By living simply, I hope to gain more time with family, the possibility of raising children and staying at home, and moving more thoughtfully through life. I have been working towards spending less and reducing debt, and I am no longer concerned with keeping up with what others are doing."

— *Shannon, Florida—Full-time Attorney*

"Simplicity means living a life that doesn't require excesses of anything. We live in the country and grow a lot of our own foods. We eat whole grains, and do food storage so we don't have to make frequent trips to town. I am learning to make clothing for our children and for myself. We keep our "stuff" to a minimum. We live in a relatively small home for our area, and only own one car. This is all to be better stewards of what the Lord provides for us.

"At first, our desire to simplify was motivated by our decision for me to be a stay-at-home mom when I was pregnant with our oldest daughter. Frugality became a necessity as our income was cut more than half due to my loss of income and my husband's change in jobs. It was tough, but we made it. Now that we don't have to be frugal for financial reasons, we have chosen a life of simplicity. We choose to be frugal with our resources, time and energy so we can use our extra resources to minister to others."

— *Lori S., California—Homemaker*

"Simplicity means having a lot of free time on the weekends to enjoy life: simple meals, simple clothes (little dry cleaning and ironing), simple make-up, simple shoes. I was tired of rushing home from work and eating dinner late, doing mounds of dishes every night, spending weekends shopping and running errands. We want to retire in ten years (when I'm 47), at the same time our nine-year-old will be starting college. We also want to enjoy life along the way.

"Our decision to simplify started several years ago with my husband saying he felt our weekends were spent shopping and running errands. We bought an inexpensive old camping trailer and started camping frequently, getting out of the 'Let's buy!' rut.

"By simplifying our lives, we've gained substantial savings, we eat nutritiously at almost every meal, our grocery savings are considerable, we spend less money on clothing, our camping vacations are fun and frugal and our home is lovely.

"Several years ago, I was a suits-and-high heels wearing, highly stressed, uptight, over-worked and overwhelmed wife and mother. Now, I'm sitting here writing this in my denim jumper and flat shoes. My life is much simpler, and I am much happier."

—Becky M., California—Human Resources Manager

"I've come to the conclusion that I am the only person who can protect my children and my husband from the frenetic pace of modern life and the agitated bad-tempered attitudes that sometimes seem to accompany this lifestyle. I actively choose to center our lives around home, church, family and friends and no longer concern myself with anyone else's opinion of my 'wasted career' (advanced graduate degree and abandoned high-power career) or seemingly old-fashioned values. In my opinion, there's nothing more modern than this yearning for simplicity and peace.

"I'm motivated by purely selfish needs to remain sane and stable for the sake of my family. I refuse to be torn apart by feeling that I should go 85 directions at once and like it! My children are not going to be stressed out either; my husband and I are careful to only schedule a very few activities for them. We feel that they should be free to be children and that means dancing in the flower borders around the yard and throwing mulch some days.

"I was confined to bed for two extremely close pregnancies and I decided that I had to simplify just to survive. We hoped to preserve sanity. We have far exceeded our own expectations, and now have friends and strangers who comment on our happy life and well-adjusted children.

"I have occasionally allowed the opinions of former colleagues and professional women to make me feel inadequate or even guilty about my decisions. I mentioned this to a friend of mine who left her veterinary practice to raise a family and her response was, "Why should we have to feel pressure to contribute to the Gross National Product?' When I stopped laughing, the feelings of discontentment were gone. I keep that idea close, to beat back the lurking self-doubts. The best solution to almost any problem is probably found in the laughter of friends.

I gave up a career that I loved in order to take the most challenging, rewarding career I can imagine. I will not regret having given up some freedom and career rewards when I am older. My husband and children are my first priority, and I'm happier than I've ever been."

—*Catherine F., Virginia—Full-time mother*

"We've chosen simplicity in most areas of life because life is too short to spend time on things that don't or won't eventually bring us happiness. The desire to find a way to be home to raise my daughter full-time was the clincher. I couldn't bear the idea of leaving our baby, life's most precious gift, to the care of someone else. It was a very difficult and guilt-ridden decision to quite my job and change our lifestyle so drastically. Following a budget and learning to live without some of the things we want hasn't been easy, but it has been worth it!

"I hated working in a corporate environment. There were many monetary rewards for the hard work, but I felt smothered and discouraged by the jealousy and misplaced values of people around me. I felt that no matter how hard I worked, I was only contributing to the wealth of the company and not to the welfare and growth of people. This caused me a great deal of emotional, physical and spiritual stress.

But it helped to teach me that my priority and most-valued thing in life is my family.

"As a shop-o-holic, it's been very hard to not spend a lot of money on clothes and household items. I used to take pride in the bargains I would find and feel like I'd accomplished a lot in a successful shopping trip. Now I take pride in every day that I don't spend any money at all, not even on a bargain. Most importantly, I now spend time with my family."

—Lora R., North Carolina—Full-time wife and mother

"Simplicity means not rushing around fulfilling everyone else's priorities. Simplicity involves investing myself, my family and our resources in important things, rather than short-lived pleasures. While I finished work on my MA, I worked with international students. It has long been my desire to provide funds to assist poor students in their education. I hope to be able to fund full-time scholarships. These students work so hard for so little, and we in comparison have so much.

"My husband and I are slowly redoing our 100-year-old home. This has been a great hobby for me, and I've learned that under-decorated houses can be more comfortable than matched-set places. I also love gardening in season. We get all our vegetables from the garden and armloads of flowers.

"The longer we go without, the easier it is to forget why something was ever essential. We don't miss TV, restaurants or anything else that we consciously do without.

"My husband used to be a major spend-thrift, as a single guy on a tenured professor's salary. However, after two years of marriage, we had $30,000 in the bank, and he'd never noticed what I had been sneaking from checking into savings. This money permitted him to take a six-month leave of absence without pay, and also go to Europe for six weeks. He's been a convert ever since. He's looking forward to a frugally-induced early retirement."

— Lynn C., Missouri—University Academic Advisor

"Simplicity means discovering what is important to one's self, and making that the focus of life, not spending time on insignificant pursuits. I was motivated to live simply by seeing how empty people's lives are, who are concerned with always having more, or the latest. I want to be more content with my life, not always striving to want more materialistic things, and cluttering my life with junk. I've also grown to understand that a simple, rather than extravagant, lifestyle is in line with my faith. Simplicity provides a clarity of purpose. It allows for less time to take care of material possessions. It creates more time to spend with people and activities that matter to me. It encourages freedom from debt."

— Amy, Pennsylvania—Customer Service
Representative and Pastor's wife

"Simplicity means living in the least complicated way possible. It means making the most out of the least. It means complete honesty and truth. I am trying to simplify every aspect of my life. It began with weaning away from materialism over a twenty-year time span. The 'Back to the Land' movement of the 1970's first inspired me. The idea of living off the grid and being more self-sufficient really caught my attention. I knew we couldn't up and sell the house and move to a homestead, so I tried to do everything I could on our suburban, almost-quarter-acre lot, with small tract house. We couldn't have livestock or chickens, but I could get the best buy for our money and use it efficiently.

"I learned to bake our own healthy breads, grow a small garden for vegetables and plant fruit trees. I bought a hand mill and 200 pounds of wheat, and learned to mill my own flour. I buy used books that teach me a better way of doing something. I buy classic literature for my home library (used, of course). I am culling my wardrobe down to just the items I will wear in a week. I've found that comfortable tennis shoes and high-tech hiking boots go with all manor of denim skirts and jumpers. My hair is graying and long enough for a bun (no salon styling expense or hair spray). I rarely wear make-up. I buy nothing that has to be dry cleaned. I cut my husband's hair (he is so brave!), and we make most gifts and cards.

"The book *Diet for a Small Planet* impressed me and motivated us to eat more conservatively. Not using cosmetics, hair sprays and other chemical concoctions helps just a tiny bit to keep the air clean, but we believe that it's worth it. We have always had fuel efficient cars. We have always walked when able.

"I have come to the knowledge that God instructs us to live simply in our everyday dealings, and be rich in love, compassion, charity and witness. Character cannot be bought, only learned. Our simple wisdom will teach the upcoming generation how to best survive without being dependent on the wrong people, things and ideas. My children renew my spirit, and now my grandchildren renew me.

"It's mainly my Christian faith that has motivated me to live simply. In all good conscience, I can't purposely gather more than I need. The benefits I receive from living simply are a clear conscience, and knowing that I am doing the best I can to make our lives easier and less stressful."

—Linda V., California—Full-time homemaker

"Simplicity means getting back to the basics. Doing away with non-essentials like matching furniture sets for the house, name-brand goods, electronic gismos, larger television screens. Really evaluating the priorities in life, making a conscious effort to question everything—purchases, diet, values.

"Simplicity allows me to focus more on the essential things in life. It also grants me control over the way I live. Often we become distracted by the material things in this world.

"For me choosing to live simply involved a refocusing of priorities in life. First, I recognized that there were certain things I hoped to achieve (setting up a home, further studies, able to provide for family, build up nest egg). Then I reminded myself that the resources I have are limited. I was also determined to avoid personal loans. Eventually I had to sit down and decide which goals were short term and which were long term. It was the logical realization that you couldn't have everything you want. I suppose you can call that voluntary simplicity. I find that life becomes so complicated when you believe that every thing is equally important to you, you can't do without this, or you can't do without that. You allow yourself to be persuaded by family members, friends and advertisements that you have to own certain things (like a larger car, latest handphone model, hottest nail polish color). Ultimately, if you examine your life, you'll realize that these extras are just that, extras."

—Eveline H., Singapore— Administrator

"To me, simplicity means easy, without difficulty or hassles. I've chosen to simplify my life in the area of household chores and meals. I went through a career change, which required several years of schooling while raising two small children, so the easier, the better. I have an extremely busy life. I work two jobs and have two active children who use me as their personal chauffer.

"I wanted it all, without taking quality and quantity of lifestyle away from my children, I wanted them to know I loved them and wanted to spend as much time with them as I could. I was determined to have social, mental and emotionally stable/happy children, regardless of the fact that their father and I no longer lived under the same roof. There was no longer time for a 'spotless' house or time for perfect lengthy meals. I did not have a lot of time to spend on laundry and darning, because I needed that time to spend with my kids. The only thing that shows the sacrifices is the house—it looks lived in.

"Over the past two years I've experienced 'difficult' health, and there are times when I am emotionally and physically exhausted. I don't have the energy or time to concentrate on the small stuff. I live by the saying, 'Don't sweat the small stuff. . . and most everything is small stuff.'"

—Darlene S., Virginia—Registered Nurse and single mother

"Simplicity to me is finding the easiest and least expensive way to achieve the best results. I did some research and almost cried when I realized how much we were wasting. I hate to be wasteful. I hate to squander money. I hate the hustle and bustle of keeping up with the Joneses. We now have more money in our savings, and I enjoy life better.

"At first, my husband thought my decision to live simply and frugally was cute. 'Your little hobby,' he used to call it. I went around turning off lights, covering the windows with plastic, making grocery lists, refusing to spend an extra $1.50 on brownie mix from the store. Then when he lost his job last year, he realized that I saved us a lot of money and he became more supportive. I showed him how much we saved per year by just changing things slightly. For instance, signing up for free Internet and the cheapest cable for our television saves us almost $400 per year, and taking a bottle of homemade iced tea instead of buying a coke from the machines saves us $80 per year.

"Last summer, we bought a house in need of lots of work in the nicest neighborhood in the city. All the house needed was some painting and some cosmetic work (new carpets, etc.). We wanted to do most of the work ourselves. I used the library, the Internet, the helpful people at our local hardware store, and found the easiest ways to update our house inexpensively.

"It hasn't been easy. However, I would rather learn how to do something myself, than to pay someone else to do it. I would rather spend an hour of hard labor doing something myself, than spend four hours working at my job to make enough money to hire someone else to do the labor for an hour."
— *Ashley C., Tennessee*

"Simplicity means a lack of complications that'll drive you crazy. It means not desiring 'stuff' that only strokes those wounded parts that really do need to be healed, not stroked with purchases to make you feel worthy. Not being in bondage to the prevailing winds of purchasing, leasing, charging, etc. I live simply because I guess I've just been 'bent' that way. Stuff offends me. It is extremely distasteful to me. I used to clean and organize houses, and the two I worked on the most were quite large and quite stuffed with 'stroke' purchases.

"I have lived simply ever since I had any say in it. I even lived in a mining shack with two dogs and a cat for a while, no water, no plumbing/sewage, no electricity. It was cold! But the freedom from stuff was just wonderful. We now live (four of us and a cat) in a 1600 square foot house that we purchased 19 years ago feeling it was too large. We used the living room and den as a workshop (my husband is a carpenter) until six years ago, now we are struggling to deal with the thought of appearing normal—with a semi-formal living room now.

"Simplifying our lives has provided more financial freedom. We also have less stress, less junk to take care of, less stuff to do and we have more time. I think simplifying had more to do with discovering just who I am and what I really care about. *The Artist's Way* by Julia Cameron has seriously helped in that respect.

"I recently realized that I was groomed from way back to be a simple-freak when I lived in a two-room cabin for awhile as a child. Trotting out to the outhouse in the snow late at night was not much fun, but you didn't have to clean it. Later, I chose to live in a tiny mining shack just to see how simple I could get. It was a wonderful time but a better wood stove would've been a nice thing to have had. I have come to appreciate heat, and now that I live in the south, I really like air-conditioning as well. But the simplicity honed in me from way back is a special thing that I have come to see as a major blessing."

— *Stevie Ann A., South Carolina—Homeschooling mom*

"Simplicity means stopping to think, 'Will this matter in five years? Will this add to or detract from time with my family? Is this a true need or want? Am I doing this out of guilt or because I feel it's truly what I should do?' Stopping to think about these things before doing or buying something has helped me to focus on my priorities.

"As a home school mom of three young children, time is my most valuable resource. Time spent out of the home (or even in the home watching television, compulsively cleaning, reading trash, etc.), means less time with my family. I've been motivated to live simply by the idea that in a short time my kids will be grown and gone. It's time I will never be able to get back. I will always be able to buy a new car, decorate my house, take a class, etc., later. Someday, all of our possessions will be gone when we die, and I'm certain the kids won't remember what toy they got for Christmas or what kind of car we drove. What they will remember is the time that we spent together as a family.

"By living simply and frugally, I can stay home with my children and still enjoy the little splurges that make life sweeter. If we don't spend money on fast food several times a week, it means my husband and I can eat at a nice romantic restaurant once a month. If we don't spend money on every new toy that comes on the market, we can afford a new computer. There are always choices to be made about how to spend our money, and we've found that by limiting the junk, we can afford more quality in our lives.

"There are always choices to be made in life. Do I buy the red dress or the blue one? Not buying the blue dress isn't a sacrifice—it's a choice. I see others that strive to keep up with the Joneses and how much time and energy is preoccupied with either getting the latest thing or having to pay for it. Leaving that lifestyle behind is not a sacrifice. It's a choice.

"I am fortunate that money is not a pressing issue for our family, the way it is for some. I believe that is due in large part because of spending choices we've made. In filling this survey out, I realize that some people are frugal because they have no choice. It's not a matter of choosing Mexico over the Grand Canyon for a vacation, it's choosing food over laundry soap. I don't want to minimize real financial struggles in any way, but I would like to point out that the majority of people we know are in the same middle class bracket as ourselves. I see them tottering on the brink of financial disaster because of incredibly foolish spending decisions. Most of them look at me like I'm nuts when I share that aside from the house, we're debt free. It really does boil down to deciding: Is this item something I really need, or is it something I simply want? I think that if each of us sat down and considered what is a true need, and how much of our life is filled with wants, we would be amazed."

—Gwynne T., Washington—Homemaker/Seamstress

"To me, simplicity does not necessarily mean more convenient or taking less time, although it could. It involves anything that takes a bit of the complication out of my life, be it emotional, financial or practical. It involves making conscious personal choices. Simplicity allows me to stop and smell the flowers, to remember what's really important. I have taken up gardening. Gardening hasn't brought simplicity to my life because it saves me time—it doesn't !However, it brings to my life a sense of serenity and connection with the world outside of my television or computer screen. It eases daily stress and gives me pleasure.

"In today's world, it's too easy to get swept along with the tide of life, and look back years later and wonder what you did with your time. I'd like to know that I'm not getting swept along blindly, and instead am making conscious choices about what I do with my time, money and energy.

"For the most part, I think simplicity has been good for me because it's helped me to see what matters, and what doesn't, in life."

— Cathleen, Ontario Canada

"Simplicity means that I have fewer possessions, which means less time and money spent caring for them, which means more time to pursue recreational activities and spend time with friends and family.

"I have gotten rid of about 60% of my possessions, and kept only those that I truly use and/or love. I am actually much happier this way, but for a while I was caught on the "buy, buy, buy" merry-go-round. Since I have reduced my possessions, it takes me about five minutes each evening to pick up and clean my apartment whereas it used to take me at least 45 minutes or more—mostly because there wasn't room to actually put anything away.

"There are more important ways to spend my life other than caring for possessions. I like to have dinner with friends, play in the park with my niece, walk by the river or just sit and watch the clouds. Of course, coming home and being able to walk around without tripping or stepping over anything and always knowing where everything is has definitely been a selling point for me.

"Material things don't make me happy; things only make me want more things. If things are not what I value in life, I should not be spending the majority of my time buying, admiring, storing, dusting, moving and reorganizing things. Someone once told me to imagine that I'm 90 years old and looking back on my life. From this frame of mind, what was most important and what was least important? They told me to spend more time and energy on what matters to me most, and less (or not at all) on what is not important. When I am 90, I imagine I will look back most fondly on the times I have shared with other people, and the adventures that I have had; I doubt that I will care whether I had a name-brand stereo or enough knickknacks to fill the top of my bookshelf.

"By choosing simplicity, I hoped to gain the time and freedom to pursue my dreams and have fun. This has certainly become my reality. In addition, I have found more inner peace; the part of my being that used to worry about all the 'stuff' and 'having, having, having' has been freed."

—*Kathi C., California—Teacher*

"Simplicity means doing things in such a way that they require less money, time and effort to get positive results. We try to use simplicity in each area of our life. We have always been careful of our resources, and have tried to conserve, reduce, reuse and recycle everything. We live this way partly out of necessity after making some mistakes with debt in the recent past. We have downsized to conform to a realistic budget so that we can live without having to use further credit. We have been married for thirteen years and have practiced simplicity since shortly before our son was born. This allowed me to stay home full-time until our son was of school age.

"The benefits gained from living more simply are many, and continue to show themselves. Because I now cook ahead for the freezer, I have more time to spend with my family, working on chores, or just sitting and talking instead of always rushing and never having dinner ready, or just running out for a bite to eat.

"My husband has not always been supportive. I finally put all of our expenses for a year down on paper and showed him. 'This is our income; this is what we spend on housing and utilities and taxes, this is food and doctor, this is the 'I have no clue' amount (which was very large).' Once he saw that, and saw an actual budget and how we could stay within our income and slowly pay off our credit card debt, he came over to the way of simplicity."

—*Catherine M., Wisconsin—Part-time Cashier*

"Simplicity to me means de-cluttering one's life physically, emotional and spiritually. I think simplicity enhances life, not restricts it. Modest dress is important to me. Being Muslim, I wear long dresses and scarves when I go out. In the West, this is seen as restricting. On the contrary, I find it quite liberating. I am not a slave to fashion designers whims. I've also always been a person who can appreciate things without having to own them. I believe we make things harder for ourselves by being ungrateful and looking for more than what is necessary. If we put God and family first, all the rest will fall into place."

—*Sheree E., Cairo Egypt—Mother of eight*

"Simplicity means no longer being in the 'rat race' of life. I was a Systems Analyst of a life insurance company for years until I realized my career was wrecking my home life. I quit my job to try and live simply and frugally. Simplicity to me means making home-cooked meals from scratch, not buying the latest trendy clothes, not thinking you have to be doing some activity every waking hour of the day.

"My decision to stay at home with my children has greatly improved and simplified our lives. It had gotten to the point where I was so tired and stressed out, that I couldn't function at home anymore. I hardly ever cooked, and my children were eating fast food meals two or three times per week. My children have benefited immensely from my staying home. We still tend to do a lot (soccer, church), and I'm more involved with their school (room parent), but I have more time for them. My husband especially enjoys having supper on the table when he comes in from a hard day at work.

"Living simply involves conserving our natural resources. The less one buys, the less things go to waste. I'm trying to be better at buying gently used items whenever possible, rather than new ones. My children think nothing of wearing second-hand clothes or shoes from a consignment shop because it's new to them. If someone teaches their children to be materialistic, they're setting them up for a rude awakening when the children get into the real world."

— *Tish V., Mississippi—Stay-at-home Mom*

"To me, simplicity means enjoying everything to its fullest. Taking advantage of a spring day to teach my daughter about trees, or being calmed by a light rain. Simplicity means looking at the simple methods of living. It means creating your own clothes and supplies, growing your own food, and taking advantage of what nature provides for us.

"I was motivated to live simply after having my daughter and realizing there must be something better than working 40 hours a week and having no time to enjoy my family, my garden and no time to learn new things. Simple living makes sense to me. It coincides with my life goals of being a good mom, wife and a good student. I want to learn as much as I can and give back what I can to others while still having enough for my family.

"I have listed my life goals, and have created goal posters with pictures, words and ideas of things I want to be or want to know. This creates more focus and helps me evaluate the time I spend on different things. I ask myself, 'Is what I'm doing right now helping me achieve my goals? If not, why am I spending precious time, energy and resources on it?'

"For me, simplicity has been organizing my priorities and keeping goals in mind as I live each day. I don't ever want to look back on my life and say, 'I wish I did...' whatever. I take advantage of every moment and look for the beauty of everything. I've found that when I pay more attention to the world around me, there is something new and beautiful to look at each day. I'm learning so much more and have become a much more empathetic person. I use the money that we have for others by buying toys for a local daycare with disadvantaged children or sending money to the Boys and Girls Club. I am a more positive person to be around I feel good about each day when I go to sleep.

—*Kari T., Washington, Part-time Teacher and Small Business Owner*

Bibliography

Back to Basics. Reader's Digest Association, 1981.

Ban Breathnach, Sarah. *Simple Abundance*. Warner Books, Inc., 1995.

Barfield, Rhonda. *15-Minute Cooking*. Lilac Publishing, 1998.

Barfield, Rhonda. *Eat Healthy for $50 a Week*. Lilac Publishing, 1996.

Barnes, Emilie. *More Hours in My Day*. Harvest House Publishers, 1994.

Better Homes and Gardens Make-Ahead Cookbook. Meredith Corporation, 1971.

Better Homes and Gardens Fix & Freeze Cookbook. Meredith Corporation, 1986.

Blue, Ron. *Master Your Money*. Thomas Nelson, 1997.

Bower, Dee Sarton and Mary Eileen Wells. *Homemade to Go*. Purrfect Publishing, Ltd., 1997.

Bredenberg, Jeff. *Clean it Fast, Clean it Right*. Rodale Press, Inc., 1998.

Burkett, Larry. *The Financial Planning Workbook*. Moody Press, 1990.

Burkett, Larry. *Women Leaving the Workplace*. Moody Press, 1999.

Burton, Linda et all. *What's a Smart Woman Like You Doing at Home?* United States: Mothers At Home, 1992.

Carney, Mary. *Looking Well to the Ways of Your Household*. Simple Living Workshops, 1997.

Case, Richard et all. *The Money Diet*. Spire, 1995.

Chidester, Jane E and John L. Macko. *Budget Yes*. Tulip Tree Press, 1997.

Chilton, David. *The Wealthy Barber*. Prima Publishing, 1991.

Clarkson, Sally. *Seasons of a Mother's Heart*. Whole Heart Ministries, 1998.

Cloninger, Claire. *A Place Called Simplicity*. Harvest House Publishers, 1993.

Comstock, Anna Botsford. *Handbook of Nature Study*. Cornell University Press, 1974.

Covey, Stephen R. *The Seven Habits of Highly Effective Families*. Golden Books, 1997.

Cox, Connie and Chris Evatt. *30 Days to a Simpler Life*. Plume, 1998.

Culp, Stephanie. *How to Get Organized When You Don't Have the Time*. Writer's Digest Books, 1986.

Dacyczyn, Amy. *The Complete Tightwad Gazette.* Random House, 1999.

Dappen, Andy. *Shattering the Two-Income Myth.* United States: Brier Books, 1997.

Dean, Athena. Consumed by Success. United States: *Wine Press Publishing,* 1995.

Diehn, Gwen and Terry Krautwurst. *Nature Crafts for Kids.* United States: Sterling Publishing Co., Inc., 1992.

Dominguez, Joe and Vicki Robin. *Your Money or Your Life,* New Edition. United States: Penguin USA, 1999.

Elgin, Duane. Voluntary Simplicity. United States: Quill, 1993.

Emery, Carla. *The Encyclopedia of Country Living.* Seattle: Sasquatch Books, 1994.

Farm Journal *Freezing & Canning Cookbook.* New York: Doubleday & Company, Inc., 1973.

Fleming, Jean. *Finding Focus in a Whirlwind World.* Fort Collins, Colorado: Treasure Ministry Resources, 1991.

Fuller, Cheri. *Home-Life.* United States: Honor Books, 1988.

Gore, Michael. 2001 *Household Hints and Dollar Stretchers.* New York: Hanover House, 1957.

Hastings, Betty-Anne with Mary-Beth Connors. *Betty-Anne's Helpful House-hold Hints.* New York City: Ventura Books, 1982.

Heloise. *Heloise's Housekeeping Hints.* New York: Pocket Books, 1965.

Heloise. *Heloise's Kitchen Hints.* New York: Simon & Schuster, 1963.

Heloise. *Hints from Heloise.* United States: Arbor House Publishing Company, 1980.

Hickerson, Neva. *Pioneer Crafts for Kids.* Ventura, California: Gospel Light, 1991.

Horowitz, Shel. *The Penny-Pinching Hedonist.* AWM, 1995.

Hough, Deborah. *Simple Living.* Simple Pleasures Press, 1996.

Hunt, Mary. *Cheapskate in the Kitchen.* St. Martin's Paperbacks, 1997.

Hunt, Mary. *The Complete Cheapskate.* Broadman & Holman Publishers, 1998.

Hunt, Mary. *The Cheapskate Monthly Money-Makeover.* St. Martin's Paperbacks, 1995.

Hunt, Mary. *Debt-Proof Your Holidays.* St. Martin's Paperbacks, 1997.

Jogerst, Karen. *If I Could Just Get Organized*. Rubies Publishing, 1999.

Kenyon, Mary Potter. *Home Schooling from Scratch*. Gazelle Publications, 1996.

King, June. *Household Hints*. Santa Monica Press, 1994.

Levine, Karen. *Keeping Life Simple*. Storey Books, 1996.

Levison, Catherine. *A Charlotte Mason Education*. Champion Press, Ltd, 2000.

Levison, Catherine. *More Charlotte Mason Education*. Champion Press, Ltd, 2000.

Lindbergh, Anne Morrow. *Gift from the Sea*. Vintage Books, 1991.

Mains, Karen Burton. *Open Heart, Open Home*. David C. Cook Publishing Company, 1976.

McCoy, Jonni. *Frugal Families*. Holly Hall Publications, 1998.

McCoy, Jonni. *Miserly Moms*. Full Quart Press, 1996.

Milford, Susan. *The Kids' Nature Book*. Williamson Publishing Co., 1989.

Miller, Lewellyn. *The Joy of Christmas*. Bobbs-Merrill Company, Inc., 1960.

Morgan, Melissa L. and Judith Waite Allee. *Home Schooling on a Shoe String*. Harold Shaw Publishers, 1999.

Munger, Evelyn Moats and Susan Jane Bowdon. *The New Beyond Peek-a-Boo and Pat-a-Cake*. New Century Publishers, 1986.

Noel, Brook. *Back to Basics.* Champion Press, Ltd., 1999.

Noel, Brook. *The Single Parent Resource*. Champion Press, Ltd., 1998.

Norris, Gunilla. *Being Home*. Bell Tower, 1991.

Petrash, Carol. *Earthways*. Gryphon House, 1992.

Pond, Jonathan. *1,001 Ways to Cut Your Expenses*. Dell Books, 1992.

Robinson, Jo and Jean Coppock Staeheli. *Unplug the Christmas Machine*. William Morrow and Company, Inc., 1982.

Schaeffer, Edith. *The Hidden Art of Homemaking*. Tyndale House, 1971.

Shimer, Porter. *Keeping Fitness Simple*. Storey Books, 1998.

Smallin, Donna. *Unclutter Your Home*. Storey Books, 1999.

Swenson, Richard A. *Margin.* NavPress, 1992.

Taylor-Hough, Deborah. *Frozen Assets: How to Cook for a Day and Eat for a Month*. Champion Press, Ltd., 1999.

Waldo, Myra. Cooking for the Freezer. Doubleday, 1961.

Watson, Thomas. *The Art of Divine Contentment*. Soli Deo Gloria Publishing, 1653.

Winston, Stephanie. *Getting Organized*. Warner Books, Inc, 1978.

Yorkey, Mike. *Saving Money Any Way You Can*. Servant Publications, 1994.

Also available from Champion Press, Ltd...

Frozen Assets:
how to cook for a day
and eat for a month

by Deborah Taylor-Hough
ISBN: 1-891400-61-4 $14.95

Frozen Assets offers a step-by-step plan for spending less time in the kitchen without sacrificing nutrition value. By using these methods one can spend just one day in the kitchen each month and still enjoy a homemade meal for breakfast, lunch and *dinner—every day of the month*! The book contains a complete outline for those looking to benefit from this cooking revolution. With a two-week plan a one-month plan and a ten-day plan to avoid cooking over the holidays, this book is the answer to the prayers of many families seeking remedies that save time and money. Complete with shopping lists, low-fat tips, ideas for singles, instruction for adapting your own recipes and freezing guidelines, the book is the one-stop resource for those looking to increase their time at the family table and decrease their time in the kitchen and drive-through lanes.

---

365 Quick, Easy and Inexpensive Dinner Menus
by Penny E. Stone
ISBN: 1-891400-33-9 $19.95

365 Quick, Easy and Inexpensive Dinner Menus meets all the needs of every home cook. This new release tastefully combines nutrition, ease of preparation and cost-efficiency while offering not just single dish recipes but full meal *menus—one for every day of the year*! With homespun charm, warm wit and playful trivia, home-cooks are provided with a ready-made plan for entire meals that are fun, cheap and quick. *365 Quick, Easy and Inexpensive Dinner Menus* is a cookbook for the entire family and its innovative menus have been approved by kids nationwide. The book is multi-indexed: by food category and by preparation time.

Back to Basics

101 Ideas for Stengthening The Family
by Brook Noel
ISBN: 1-891400-48-7 $13.95

"Life is what happens while we're making other plans," the adage goes, but how far have modern families let that attitude take root? Too far, it would seem, when a recent survey found that the average working mother spends 50 minutes a day with her child. The average working father? Nine! It doesn't have to be. In her new book, author Brook Noel confronts the issues that continue to tear at the modern social fabric. Noel's collection of insights offer a much-needed road map back to the values that are the foundation for strong homes and strong families.

A Charlotte Mason Education $8.95
More Charltte Mason Education $13.95
by Catherine Levison

The immensely popular ideas of Charlotte Mason have inspired educators for many decades. Her unique methodology as written about in her six-volume series established the necessary protocols for an education above and beyond that which can be found in traditional classroom settings. In *A Charlotte Mason Education*, Catherine Levison has collected the key points of Charlotte Mason's methods and presents them in a simple, straightforward way that will allow families to quickly maximize the opportunities of homeschooling. With weekly schedules, a challenging and diverse curriculum will both inspire and educate your child. *A Charlotte Mason Education* is the latest tool for parents seeking the best education for their children.

I Wasn't Ready to Say Goodbye:
surviving, coping and healing
after the sudden death of a loved one
by Brook Noel and Pamela D. Blair, Ph.D.

Each year about eight million Americans suffer the death of a close family member. The list of high visibility disasters, human suffering and sudden loss is long and will continue to grow. From TWA Flight 800 to Egypt Air, from Oklahoma City to Columbine, daily we face incomprehensible loss. Outside the publicized tragedies there are many families and individuals that are suffering behind closed doors in our neighborhoods, in our own homes, in hospital waiting rooms. Now for those who face the challenges of sudden death, there is a hand to hold. *I Wasn't Ready to Say Good-bye* is the first book to devote all its pages to the unique challenges of sudden loss, written by two women who have walked the path. They cover such difficult topics as the first few weeks, suicide, death of a child, when a body isn't found, children and grief, funerals and rituals, physical effects, homicide, depression and many others.

THE SINGLE PARENT RESOURCE

FINALLY! THE PROVEN ANSWERS SINGLE PARENTS NEED

by Brook Noel with Art Klein
ISBN: 1-891400-44-4 $13.95

What kind of help do single parents need most in their day-to-day lives? The authors asked that question to over 500 single parents. Now they provide the answers to the top concerns, problems and challenges of single-parent life. Here they are—practicaly, concise, timely, relevant—and never before available in a single guide!

GETTING UP, GETTING OVER, GETTING ON
A TWELVE STEP GUIDE TO DIVORCE RECOVERY

by Micki McWade
ISBN: 1-891400-13-4 $14.95

For 20 million Americans the long process of healing after the devastation of divorce began with a single step. Most found their way alone, making mistakes and trying to reinvent their lives through trial and error. Now, borrowing the wisdom gained in the development of 12 Step Programs, this new book offers learned and proven support. Author Micki McWade adapts the best techniques, information and life lessons of long established recovery programs to provide a concise and comprehensive pathway to a fulfilling life after divorce. Whether during the painful days of the divorce itself or in the adaptive weeks and months that follow, McWade offers valuable ideas that work in relationships with children, with in-laws, and with (ex) spouses. Readers are also provided with step-by-step encouragement for forming their own support groups

---

EDUCATIONAL AND GROUP DISCOUNTS ARE AVAILABLE FOR MORE INFORMATION WRITE TO CHAMPION PRESS, LTD.

Order Form

Use this form to order the Champion books of your choice or order on-line at our web site, www.championpress.com.

QUANTITY   TITLE   PRICE

_____   _____   _____

_____   _____   _____

_____   _____   _____

_____   _____   _____

_____   _____   _____

_____ Shipping and handling. $3.95 for the first book and $1 more for each additional book

_____ Payment enclosed

_____ Please charge my ___ Visa ___ MasterCard

Account Number _____

Expiration Date _____

Signature _____

Name as it appears on card _____

Name _____

Address _____

City _____ State _____ Zip _____

Day Phone _____

MAIL FORM TO:

Champion Press, Ltd.

Suite 207

13023 NE Highway 99, #7

Vancouver WA 98686

or fax to (360) 574 4079

Visit Deborah Taylor-Hough's
web site at

www.simplemom.com

Visit the Champion Press, Ltd.
web site for all
the latest book and author news!

www.championpress.com